PRAISE FOR JASON (

"A futuristic dystopian rock ...., ..., ...
rollicking book is as unlikely, audacious, and ingenious
as the premise suggests."—*New York Times*

"A wondrous novel written entirely in heroic couplets."
—Ron Charles, *Washington Post*

"Strange and affectionate, like *Almost Famous* penned by
Shakespeare. A love letter to music in all its myriad
iterations."—*Kirkus Reviews*

"Guriel's bountiful celebration of connections between art
finds an inspiring, infectious groove."—*Publishers Weekly*

"*Forgotten Work* could be the most singular novel-in-verse
since Vikram Seth's *The Golden Gate*. Thanks to Jason
Guriel's dexterity in metaphor-making, I found myself
stopping and rereading every five lines or so, to affirm my
surprise and delight."—Stephen Metcalf

"This book has no business being as good as it is. Heroic
couplets in the twenty-first century? It's not a promising
idea, but *Forgotten Work* is intelligent, fluent, funny, and
wholly original. I can't believe it exists."—Christian Wiman

"Like the bumblebee that flies even though it shouldn't
be able to, *Forgotten Work*'s amalgam of epic poem, sci-fi
novel, and deep dive into rock-fandom gets improbably
airborne, a feat attributable not only to its author's large
and multifaceted talent, but also to his winning infatu-
ation with the diverse realms his story inhabits."
—Daniel Brown, *Literary Matters*

OTHER BOOKS BY JASON GURIEL

Technicolored
Pure Product
*The Pigheaded Soul: Essays and Reviews on Poetry
    and Culture*
Satisfying Clicking Sound
Forgotten Work

JASON GURIEL

On
Browsing

BIBLIOASIS
Windsor, Ontario

FIRST EDITION
10 9 8 7 6 5 4 3 2 1

Library and Archives Canada Cataloguing in Publication

Title: On browsing / Jason Guriel.
Names: Guriel, Jason, 1978- author.
Series: Field notes (Biblioasis) ; #5.
Description: Series statement: Field notes ; #5
Identifiers: Canadiana (print) 20220256829 | Canadiana (ebook)
20220256837 | ISBN 9781771965101 (softcover) | ISBN 9781771965118 (ebook)
Subjects: LCGFT: Essays.
Classification: LCC PS8613.U74 O5 2022 | DDC C814/.6—dc23

Edited by Daniel Wells
Copyedited by Rachel Ironstone
Series designed by Ingrid Paulson
Typeset by Vanessa Stauffer

Published with the generous assistance of the Canada Council for the Arts,
which last year invested $153 million to bring the arts to Canadians
throughout the country, and the financial support of the Government of
Canada. Biblioasis also acknowledges the support of the Ontario Arts Council
(OAC), an agency of the Government of Ontario, which last year funded 1,709
individual artists and 1,078 organizations in 204 communities across Ontario,
for a total of $52.1 million, and the contribution of the Government of
Ontario through the Ontario Book Publishing Tax Credit and Ontario Creates.

PRINTED AND BOUND IN CANADA

Contents

for Christie

I am still a learner, not a teacher, feeding somewhat omnivorously, browsing both stalk and leaves ...

—Henry David Thoreau, 1856

Browser History

THERE'S SOMETHING TO be said for the Blockbuster Video store of my youth. It was what we had in the suburbs, and it suited the way my mind worked. I liked encountering movies as physical objects dispersed throughout a large room, arranged down walls (where the new releases went) and along shelves (where the older stuff tarried). I suspect the image of walking through such a room will one day amuse my children.

Still, I miss browsing those chunky foxed VHS cases and, I suppose, their leaner DVD heirs. You could wander and let your eyes fall where they fell. The supply of any given video was finite, which meant you sometimes had to figure out a plan B. You had to swivel, double back, hunker down, tilt your head. You could be aimless in a Wordsworthian way. You could meander. This aisle, maybe, or that one. Couples paralyzed by indecision stood around like Vladimirs and Estragons. And this was in boring old Blockbuster, a corporate chain! Surely the better, arthouse, non-suburban video stores presented their patrons with real rabbit holes to fall into, real opportunities for reverie.

The aisles of the Blockbuster were themed, though less aggressively, less knowingly, than the rows that march relentlessly down the Netflix home page. A particular shelf didn't remember if you had selected one of its videos before and thus didn't try to push a similar title at you. The real-world tiles didn't proactively rearrange themselves in anticipation of your unique wants. In lieu of tailored algorithms, there were a few shelves given over to staff recommendations. These challenged you to ignore the new-release walls, decorated by market forces, and defer to the taste of an authority (or, at least, a part-time employee majoring in film).

It was a Blockbuster shelf that showed me a copy of *The Third Man*, the fiftieth anniversary edition on VHS. The tape came sleeved in a beguiling black-and-white cover, irising around the image of Orson Welles. I hadn't been looking for *The Third Man*—I barely knew what it was—but I'd been eyeing that cover for some time. Or had Welles been eyeing me? I took the tape home, finally, and played it.

I adored *The Third Man*. In time, I sought out *Citizen Kane*, Welles's most famous picture. The DVD came with two audio commentary tracks, one by filmmaker Peter Bogdanovich, a protégé of Welles's. Bogdanovich's weary, deep voice, speaking slowly over Kane, transfixed me. It seemed to dredge, almost reluctantly, a deep and singular store of insights and anecdotes. It was a kind of anti-podcast, pocked with sighs and silences. It was enormously attractive. I sought out other Welles films but also other DVDs that carried Bogdanovich's commentaries: *The Searchers*, *Bringing Up Baby*, and *To Catch a Thief*. For a time, I didn't watch movies so much as listen to Bogdanovich opine on the glories of the golden age of cinema. It was, I realized later, a rogue education.

My friends and I made pilgrimages to downtown Toronto, to bigger stores, like Sam the Record Man and HMV, and smaller concerns, like Vintage Video. There were hesitations, flirtations. I passed on a VHS copy of David Lynch's *Wild at Heart* and then changed my mind only to find it had wriggled out of the HMV and, worse, out of print. Vintage Video, for its part, stocked hard-to-find movies at hefty prices. Half the time—maybe most of the time—you couldn't secure what you were looking for; the gruff, likeable owner seemed to exist to assure you that the precious item you sought was long gone. Still, I walked out of there with finds that weren't, back then, easily findable: *Eraserhead*, *Chimes at Midnight*, and *Cockfighter*. One day, my friend Mitch turned up *The Night of the Hunter*; Stephen King's book about the history of horror, *Danse Macabre*, had dispatched Mitch on his own private quest for culture. It was, as the kids no longer say, good times.

Those downtown institutions—the Sam the Record Man and HMV—are gone now, of course. Vintage Video was uprooted by developers. It doesn't seem to have taken in its new location, which Google Street View reveals is now a Wine Rack.

Perhaps Netflix and other streaming services are sending young twenty-first-century minds rafting down tributaries of their own. I would love to imagine an algorithm steering these minds from an interest in the latest Wes Anderson product to a curiosity about Peter Bogdanovich's obscure, proto-Andersonian screwball delight *They All Laughed* and then on towards a taste for greater vistas, like Jean Renoir's *The Rules of the Game*.

But speed of scrolling, algorithmic assistance, and instant access weren't what my friends and I needed, even if we might've welcomed them as conveniences. We needed that long subway trip downtown. (We were the farthest stop west.) We needed the sobering disappointments and sporadic victories. We needed the longueurs that new technology seeks to close, as if abolishing boredom ever does anyone a favour. Mostly, we needed wind resistance. It took effort to cultivate our enthusiasms in a desert, but it's clear now that we took the desert's role for granted. Knowledge tends to stick when you've toiled for it.

* * *

"Information moves, or we move to it," wrote sci-fi novelist Neal Stephenson in *Wired* magazine, back in 1996. "Moving to it has rarely been popular and is growing unfashionable; nowadays we demand that the information come to us."

How hoary the old pathways look to us now, like ruts left by a stagecoach. What elaborate workarounds and wastes of time we'd evolved to find the content that now floods our phones. The sheer legwork of it all! One of my rituals, when I was downtown, was to steal into the so-called World's Biggest Bookstore (since razed for condos) and head for Music or Performing Arts or whatever the section was called. There, I'd browse the shelves for record guides to determine which albums might be worth my time (though clearly I had lots of time). Leafing through the goods was frowned upon. But there was always a well-thumbed copy of a guide that looked too battered for anyone to want, even if, like an oracle, it had entertained visitors. Anyway, I would eventually cross the street to Sam the Record Man or HMV and buy the album I'd settled on.

Scrolling has rendered this entire process—an afternoon's worth of activity—obsolete. Who needs all that tramping around cumbersome cities with boon companions? In a matter of clicks, armed mainly with a thumb, you can call up a consumer report, make your decision, and then head over to Amazon to seal the deal. You have your afternoon back. Not that you'd fill it with quiet reverie, of course; the new efficiencies merely make room for yet more scrolling.

* * *

THE PANDEMIC LOCKDOWNS shuttered many storefronts and surely reduced many holdout browsers to scrollers; there was no other way to acquire certain things. (I was especially gutted to see Soundscapes, Toronto's finest record store, close shop while I was working on this very essay.) But the Age of Scrolling had already long ago nudged the Age of Browsing off-screen.

You could watch the catastrophe, like a glacier calving, in real time. I started an undergraduate degree in 1997 and, in no particular hurry, emerged nearly a decade and a half later into a different world, with a doctorate in English. In the early days—when few of us possessed laptops and social media had yet to metastasize—I loved getting lost in the library stacks. I whiled away breaks between classes by stumbling on books that had nothing to do with my assignments. Within a decade, though, the library's patrons were conspicuously immobile: they sat along walls and in alcoves, laptops open on their laps, serenely siloed against the press of books all around. It was almost creepy. If the essay they were writing called for a quote, they could call up a PDF from an electronic journal. No physical labour required—just a cursory search, a cut and paste. The students had become scrollers, and the indifference of so many of them to the very stacks I used to haunt was heartbreaking.

When I came to have my own students, I rooted out the plagiarists merely by noticing competing quotation-mark styles—curly and straight—in the same essay. Straight marks were a clue that text had been copied from another source, converted to plain text, and pasted in. Whenever I saw that mix of curly *and* straight, I started googling passages *outside* of the quotation marks—and sometimes found that the student had smuggled in unattributed text. It was forensic crime-lab copyediting. My scrolling had uncovered theirs.

But many of the non-plagiarists had clearly pasted in passages too. (They weren't thieves; they'd merely failed to clean up their formatting.) Such passages were the kind that I would've retyped manually, from books spread open with an awkward elbow or paperweighted some other way. Passages I came by honestly—passages I felt I'd come to possess. Indeed, it was a three-hour journey, round trip, to bring them home to my PowerBook. I lived far from the university.

Back then, I hadn't worked out a high-minded, romantic philosophy about the virtues of wrangling physical media, a philosophy this book will attempt to articulate. (And later, as a tired PhD candidate trying to complete a dissertation, I saw the appeal of summoning digitized articles with a couple of keystrokes.) But as a restless younger student—still trying to pinpoint his interests and shed the suburbs—the journey to the stacks was no bother. Really. I was happy to travel hours for a book. The book gave me something to read on the way home.

* * *

THE VERB "BROWSE" originally meant "to eat buds and leaves." It shows up in the mid-fifteenth century as "brousen," which comes from "broster," an Old French word that means to sprout or bud. ("Broster" comes from "brost," which refers to a shoot or twig.)

"Browser," naturally, meant the thing that does the browsing: the nibbling animal. The noun entered the language around 1845, and the Thoreau quote that kicks off this book—"I am still a learner, not a teacher, feeding somewhat omnivorously, browsing both stalk and leaves"—appeared in 1856, a few years later. Thoreau likens himself to that original, four-legged kind of browser, but his metaphor anticipates future usage: the activity of nibbling knowledge and experience. By 1863, "browser" was being used to describe a person moving among books. Over a century later, in the early 1980s, the computer scientist Larry Tesler applied the term to a software search system he was futzing with. Today, billions of us bring up browsers when we want to sift the internet.

Etymologically, then, "browser" is a relatively recent phenomenon. But people have been shopping for pleasure for at least a few centuries. In their book *Perceptions of Retailing in Early Modern England*, Nancy Cox and Karin

Dannehl observe that shopping—as a pursuit "distinct from" mere "purchasing"—wasn't easy before the eighteenth century.

> The trappings of a modern shop, like counters and display facilities, appear often to have been absent, as were features like chairs, looking glasses, soft furnishings and lighting that would have made for comfortable and easy browsing. Probably a customer was obliged to ask to see particular articles, and even then to rely on the retailer to gauge what was likely to please. The opportunities to see, touch and feel, and to ruffle through the stock ... were almost certainly impossible in many shops.

Later, in the eighteenth and nineteenth centuries, plate-glass windows and advances in lighting improved the ability to shop—and gave rise to a more modern form of browsing.

As historians and academics make plain, browsing doesn't mean buying. In a 1983 article titled "Shopping Without Purchase: An Investigation of Consumer Browsing Behavior," the researchers Peter H. Bloch and Marsha L. Richins furrow their brows and define browsing as "the examination of a store's merchandise for recreational or informational purposes without a current intent to buy." Browsing, the literature assures us, isn't simply a prelude to consumption. The practice *itself* is fun. What's more, it can yield knowledge: roughage worthy of nibbling.

It can even boast radical properties. In Victorian England, browsing was a way for women to move about a city unchaperoned. As the journalist Jeff Guo notes, "housewives started roaming the city under the pretence of buying things. By this new definition, 'shopping' didn't always involve an actual purchase. It was about the pleasures of perusing—taking in the sights, the displays, the people."

A few decades after the Victorian period, William Moulton Marston—the psychologist and writer who created Wonder Woman—was extolling the virtues of inspecting store windows, and also wondering if women had an advantage in this field:

> Most men mistakenly assume that you look into show windows to find something to buy. Women know better. They enjoy window-shopping for its own sake. Store windows, when you look into them with pleasure-seeking eyes, are strange places full of mental adventure. They contain first clues to dozens of treasure hunts which, if you follow them, lead to as many different varieties of treasure.

Marston sees window-shopping, a species of browsing, as a workout for the brain: food for thought. "Experienced window adventurers," he tells us, "maintain that the perfect hunting ground for rare interests is the antique store, commonly called a 'junk shop'." One mind's junk, suggests the inventor of Princess Diana of Themyscira, is another's journey.

* * *

PERHAPS MARSTON WOULD be surprised to find that men now seem to dominate in certain categories of browsing, such as record shopping. Consider the veldt of the record store, as lovingly satirized in the 2000 film *High Fidelity*, an adaptation of Nick Hornby's novel. In one scene, a store clerk played by Jack Black confronts a hapless male customer. "You don't have it?" says an incredulous Black. The hapless male customer shakes his head. "*That* is perverse," says Black. "Don't tell anybody you don't own fucking *Blonde on Blonde*." Then, Black sighs. "It's gonna be okay." He presses the album on his prey.

The camera cuts to the store owner, played by John Cusack, whispering to a colleague, "I will now sell five copies of *The Three E.P.s* by The Beta Band." ("Do it," the colleague whispers back, as if participating in a crime.) Cusack pipes the CD over his store's speakers—and piques the curiosity of another male customer. The browsers, as the film depicts them, are both hunter and hunted: snobby flaneurs of the physical format, but insecure objects of attention as well. To browse is to act *and* be acted *on*: to exercise one's taste while submitting to the authority of others.

* * *

RECORD SHOPS, OF course, have dwindled—picked off by larger predators like Amazon. In 2012, the Melody Record Shop in Washington, DC, decided to close its doors for good. It had been a *force* for good and a source of authority: a beloved family-owned concern for over three decades. But online shopping had bled Melody of business. The *Washington Post* sent a journalist to cover the death throes. The critic Leon Wieseltier lamented the loss in the *New Republic*.

Halfway through his elegy, however, Wieseltier began to dilate on something he called "the time-honored intellectual and cultural activity known as browsing." His distinctions are helpful:

Browsing is to Amazon what *flaneurie* is to Google Earth. It is an immediate encounter with the actual object of curiosity. The browser (no, not that one) is the *flaneur* in a room. Browsing is not idleness; or rather, it is active idleness—an exploring capacity, a kind of questing non-instrumental behavior. Browsing is the opposite of "search." Search is precise, browsing is imprecise. When you search, you find what you were looking for; when you browse, you find what you were not looking for. Search corrects your knowledge, browsing corrects your ignorance. Search narrows, browsing enlarges. It does so by means of accidents, of unexpected adjacencies and improbable associations. On Amazon, by contrast, there are no accidents. . . . But serendipity is how the spirit is renewed; and a record store, like a bookstore, is nothing less than an institution of spiritual renewal.

How often serendipity saw to our needs back when we wandered the world without a data plan, like benighted exiles in a Bible verse. For instance, while lingering aimlessly in my university bookstore, I made a friend of a clerk, a kindred consumer of poems. And while killing time at a used bookshop in Montreal, I made another friend: *The Castle of Indolence* by Thomas Disch. As I turned its pages on the train home to Toronto, Disch's charmingly acerbic book about poetry left me changed.

How often our wanderings rewarded us. I still remember—can't *not* remember—the pale, long-haired proprietor of the Hairy Tarantula comic shop, who always looked like he'd just descended from some cross to partake of a spliff. He tolerated the loitering of me and my friends. He even opened his shelves to our wares—our homemade xeroxed comics—and actually *paid* us for them, though not without gently critiquing our approach to stapling. (Fold the pages and use a saddle stitch, was the takeaway.) Later, he invited us to take part in a mini convention for indie comic artists, at the rear of the shop. His investment in our amateur product surely added up to a loss for his business; our comics remained untouched on the shelf he reserved for local wannabes.

But what a thrill for us high school kids—to be encouraged. To be *on* a shelf. Your real-world browser history, the one your mind accumulates as you wander the world, can't ever really be erased.

In Praise of the Mall, Boredom, and Just Browsing

WHEN I WAS very young, my mother was a typist: she made copies of documents on a typewriter loaded with carbon paper, retyping every single word. (In other words, she was a monk.) My father sorted mail for Canada Post. Neither parent possessed a university degree. The now-inconvenient demands of physical matter—to be handled, organized, shuffled, fed to slots, borne off, duplicated—gave my parents a way to scratch out a living.

My sister and I were provided for, don't get me wrong. But there was no outlay for an annual holiday, for airfare and hotel. Nor was there much money for the extracurriculars of daily life—the little leagues, the skating lessons—which every other child appeared to enjoy. My parents could manage the mall, so that's where we went on the weekend.

This is how we did it.

First, we parked near a department store entrance. We never entered through the mall proper; we came at the mall obliquely, stealing in through one of its larger tenants, like the Bay or Sears. I don't know why this approach seemed important, but it did. And my father always parked far away. He didn't trust other drivers not to ding his paintwork.

By this point on the Saturday—for Saturday was the day of such trips—it was lunchtime. Thus, we made our way to the food court, a real treat given that my mom cooked throughout the week. After lunch, we typically disbanded, with a plan to meet up later.

There were variations on the ritual: sometimes my sister went with my mother; sometimes we hit China King Buffet on route. (Technically, it was China Buffet King, but we never got that right.) Also, "the mall," as I have it, was one of a few malls within driving distance. For ease of reading, I've been referring to a single, abstracted form.

But most of the time, once lunch was done, I was on my own for an hour or two. I was a teenager armed with a little bit of spending money and the freedom to roam. By "roam," I don't mean the thing your smartphone does. To roam was to be a body in motion, confronting the world in all its shaggy, unmacheted density.

What's more, there was no way, short of arranging a mall-wide announcement via intercom, for anyone to reach me. There was no way for them to change the meetup location or tell me they were going to be late. The lack of smartphones gave daily life a little edge back then.

It was the 1990s, but it might as well have been the 1390s. I had to make it to the appointed oak tree on time.

* * *

PERHAPS MY MEMORY of browsing the mall is shot through with the faintest sepia tint. I'm sure I was bored some of the time. Lunch behind me, I was typically after a specific novel or CD or comic book, which used up my spending money almost immediately and set me adrift for the remainder of the trip, until the agreed-upon meetup time. Anyway, wasn't the mall a site of vapid, capitalist consumption? Shouldn't I have been wandering an art gallery or nudging a soccer ball out of doors? By the parenting standards of today, my family's Saturdays would not be judged especially nourishing.

But at least the mall back then was modest—low ceilinged, less brilliantly lit, and compact. The scale was human and the stores affordable. They served the needs of the browser, not the brand.

The architect Victor Gruen, a socialist of all things, designed the first mall, the Southdale Center in Edina, Minnesota, which opened in 1956. Gruen envisioned the mall as an atoll of community in the pedestrian-proof suburbs. Homes would huddle around the mall, and the mall would possess all the necessary amenities: post office, library, art, what have you. In a newspaper article from the period, Gruen and economic consultant Lawrence P. Smith describe a utopian vision:

[Malls] will welcome the hordes of automobiles which approach them, providing easy access and

ample free parking space. They will offer restful-
ness, safety and esthetic values. They can become
places where suburbanites will visit for a short
shopping trip and also centers where they will
want to congregate for many hours.

With the advent of the large shopping center
there is provided a new outlet for that primary
human instinct to mingle with other humans.

Gruen's utopian vision never quite came to pass. Stok-
ing consumption became the primary goal of malls.
What's more, the department stores that anchored the
smaller original malls eventually fled for the mega malls
of the 1990s. The mega malls ate their modest forebears—
and then online shopping came for the mega malls, one
yawning whale swallowing the next. Naturally, you can
now inspect online spooky photos of empty abandoned
malls. Like *Star Trek*'s Borg, the internet coolly, ruthlessly,
assimilates the carcass.

Some of the mega malls of my childhood, like Sherway Gardens and Square One, have survived by
metastasizing. They've sprouted new wings, as cavernous as airport terminals, boasting ever-more luxurious
concerns. (They sit in the suburbs of Toronto and have
oodles of unused parking lot to work with.) The odd
time I've revisited one of these augmented malls as an
adult, I've felt scandalized, even foolish. My contem-
poraries and I had made do with so much less! Our
less-mega twentieth-century malls offered claustro-
phobic brickwork, dimly lit food courts, and
nondescript brands. Should we have been wanting
malls with Louis Vuittons all along? Or the sort of two-

story bookstores that stock pillows extolling the virtues of cottage life?

* * *

FOR THE RECORD, I liked browsing that smaller, older, dingier kind of mall on my own, even if it was sometimes boring and the corridors weren't the width of hangars. Plus, I had my father as an example.

Dad was the purest of browsers. He rarely bought anything. "Just browsing," we sometimes say when we want the sales associate to back off. Dad was always just browsing. He loved to visit expensive watches, ties, and pens in their display cases, hands clasped behind his back. He was born in 1922, could summon memories of the Great Depression, and didn't possess a credit card until late in life. If he wanted something, he saved up for it—and while he saved up for it, he visited it. To browse was not merely to *consume*. To browse was to move among beautiful objects. The mall, as Dad saw it, was something like a gallery. Sometimes, in my solo post-lunch wanderings, I would stumble on him enjoying the Rolexes and Omegas. (An awkward delight of browsing on your own was running into the person you weren't yet scheduled to meet up with.)

Browsing, I came to learn, was best when it was aimless and inefficient. It took the long way or what Dad called ironically, without fail, "the scenic route." Dad always preferred the scenic route. After a trip to the Eaton Centre, Toronto's big downtown mall, we'd inevitably go south on the subway and loop back *up* to the main line, rather than simply head north to begin with, which would've saved us a couple of stops.

Dad loved downtown. When I was still too young to break off on my own, he would drag me along to some of his cherished haunts, like Arcade Coin & Stamp Galleries and Remenyi House of Music. (He collected stamps and played the violin in his spare time.) Arcade and Remenyi were sites of serious browsing, invariably manned by older men and pickled in silence. I would wait for Dad as he leafed through swollen binders of stamps or scrutinized violins he would never buy, trussed up like lacquered ducks. Sometimes, he was after a specific stamp or, say, an E string, if he had broken one. Most of the time, he was just browsing. I had no device with which to distract myself, so I browsed too. Or circled the store like something in a tank. To be a child back then was to be in tow.

On Sundays, before the advent of Sunday shopping, Dad and I would drive to nearby Cloverdale Mall and walk *around* the locked structure. The large, empty parking lot, abutting a highway, was our Scottish Highlands. Perhaps we were engaged in a form of conceptual browsing—or anti-browsing. In any case, this activity really *was* boring. Dad dispersed stale bread for the seagulls. A few dozen metres away—you could really stretch out—I dribbled a tennis or super ball. I think my mother put me up for these missions because she worried that my father, even at his advanced age, might get up to no good. There had been trust issues, not entirely of her imagination.

* * *

I SPENT A lot of time dribbling balls as a kid. I spent a lot of time in my head. To be "in your head" is now understood to be a bad thing, but I had nowhere else to be.

Virtually no other kids lived on my street; what children there'd been had grown up and moved on, leaving behind senior citizens not quite ready yet to yield their homes to younger families. So, I'd bounce a ball against an outer wall of our bungalow, over and over, and tell myself stories, fodder for comic books I would one day letter and illustrate. (I would come to dabble in indie comics, but never got around to completing much of what I'd conceived.) I must've made a pitiful sight for Hilda, the elderly neighbour whose house faced the best wall for ball action: a boy at loose ends.

I biked a lot, too, more stories in my head. (My parents did not require me to protect the head with a helmet.) I came to like biking the same streets and alleys, over and over. Even with ten minutes left of daylight, I would roll my bike down the driveway and take a last turn around the block. I biked until August 31, 1997, when I blew a tire coming home from a friend's house. I'd gone to retrieve some physical media, my copy of Oasis's album *Be Here Now*, before the friend left for university. I was to start university, too, and soon I would be too busy to bike. The blown tire never got fixed, and the bike mouldered in the garage. I know the date of the blowout because that was the night Princess Diana died.

* * *

STILL, AS A child, and by dint of my parents' benign neglect, I learned to be okay with repetition. With boredom. I reread books, rewound vhs tapes, and browsed the same shops and shelves in malls like Cloverdale. I like to think I was preparing for a future in letters. You have to develop a deep tolerance for boredom, I tell myself. You have to have habits. The poet Kay Ryan suggests as much in her assessment of the narrow life of another poet, Stevie Smith. According to Ryan, Smith would take a glass of sherry "in the middle of every morning" with an aunt:

> And because of her life of regular habits, the rare interruption is almost hallucinogenic. She reports seeing *The Trojan Women* on a friend's television. She is nearly undone with amusement at the hash it makes of Euripides: "What an earthshaking joke this is. Yet, if my life was not simple, if I looked at television all the time, I might have missed it."
>
> Memory as a job, as a notebook to be kept, is only necessary for those who insist upon novelty. If you delight in habit as Stevie Smith did, if it is your pleasure to do things in the same way without inviting change, you don't have to write much down. And when things do change, as they will even without invitation, then you will really notice the change. Your memory will be deep, quiet, undifferentiated as a pool. Change will enter and twist like a drop of ink, the tiniest bit of new per old.

The example of Smith's insulated mind, jolted by the sudden input of television, charmed me the first time I read it. What's more, Ryan's simile—that twisting "drop of ink"—was spot on. Ryan seemed to have explained an aspect of cognition better than a neuroscientist could have. A mind whose baseline is boredom is well primed to feel, with acute sensitivity, the slightest stimuli. A mind that's buffeted by novelty, on the other hand, is the fender of a beater: it absorbs a lot of undifferentiated dings.

* * *

EVEN AFTER I'D left the suburb behind, I never quite kicked the habit, acquired from my family, of aimlessly browsing the same shops and shelves. For example, when I was a student, I was always at the York University Bookstore, trying to run out the clock before class. Later, for the better part of a decade, I worked near the University of Toronto. At lunchtime, I usually sat at my desk, ate my lunch, and looked at the internet. (In other words, I scrolled.) But quite often, with twenty minutes of lunchtime left to kill, I hustled over to the U of T Bookstore, a tempting block away. Most of the time, I had no goal, no book in mind. It was enough to be *among* books.

It was always enough to be among books, even if they were the same ones, every day. I came to know the titles at the U of T Bookstore; I came to know the contents of many stores and libraries when I had cause to be near them for a while. The familiar spines were a comfort. Plus, the occasional new spine, when it did appear, behaved like Kay Ryan's "drop of ink, the tiniest bit of new per old," blooming in my mind like dye in water.

Maybe this sounds boring, an intolerable state in the Age of Scrolling. Scrolling, after all, promises an antidote to boredom. It promises choice, abundance, novelty, diversion, *something to do*. We scroll to stave off an intolerable state. We scroll to avoid being alone with ourselves. But boredom is a natural condition, the fishbowl medium a mind should be able to swim in. In fact, research suggests that boredom is even good for the brain—for creativity, productivity, that sort of thing. My parents' benign neglect had neuroscience on its side.

Our smartphones, of course, have been designed to abolish boredom—and seize our attention with suckers. "I have two kids now and I regret every minute that I'm not paying attention to them because my smartphone has sucked me in," says Loren Brichter in a 2017 *Guardian* article. Brichter was the designer who first devised the addictive "pull-to-refresh" function for Twitter, the innovation that launched a thousand thumbs. We scroll to avoid being alone with ourselves, but we scroll, finally, because our devices have trained us to.

* * *

WHEN DAD GAVE up driving, we'd walk to Cloverdale for a slice of pizza. I had to slow my pace to match his—another longueur to endure. But Cloverdale still maintained a record shop and a Coles. Plus, I could always linger near the magazine rack in the adjoining grocery store and riffle through the *Atlantic Monthly*, as it was then called. (They've since lopped off the "*Monthly*"—progress!) There was a better newsstand in the mall proper, but the grocery store didn't hassle you. I still recall reading Caitlin Flanagan for the very first time, standing amid the clatter of shopping carts, and a wonderful David Barber poem called "Bambino Sutra."

The long hallway to the washrooms displayed photos of the mall dating back to the 1950s, when Cloverdale was open air. Eventually, management walled the mall in. In the 1980s, when I was a little kid, the interior smelled of cigarettes. Stars of daytime television made appearances. Santa Claus too. Something of Gruen's vision of community lingered in Cloverdale, like second-hand smoke. My father and other senior citizens would coalesce in the food court, nurse a coffee, and kibitz. Later, after he passed away, my mother, who had a hard time making friends, found her own strands of community there.

I've browsed Cloverdale all my life. The Coles, originally a W. H. Smith, was effectively my library. (It took too long to walk to a *real* library.) There, in the 1990s, I discovered and bought David Foster Wallace's *Infinite Jest*, a book I'd never heard of. The sudden appearance of its distinctively wide and orange spine caught my attention only because I knew the shelves of Coles as another child, with a more bucolic childhood, would've known the shoreline of his local creek. It rippled my brain, that orange spine. Another droplet of change.

Cloverdale's bakery produced the best chicken pies, and the music store always seemed to stock at least one copy of whichever album my teenage self most needed at any given moment. I'm convinced I scooped up the only copies of *Everything Must Go* and *Moseley Shoals* to ever enter that mall.

Many years later, my wife came to know the pleasures of Cloverdale when Target briefly passed through it. I enjoyed introducing her to the rest of the mall, the backdrop of my less-than-bucolic childhood. Maybe I would've preferred showing her around some scenic small-town main street. Or the football field where I'd consolidated my adolescent triumphs. But Cloverdale was what I had to show her. It was the creek I'd sloshed around in.

* * *

THE PANDEMIC HAS helped hasten the end of shopping malls. But malls have been in decline for years. Around the summer of 2020, there were about a thousand left in the United States. Research suggests that a quarter of them will close within the next five years. Amazon, naturally, is eyeing the carcasses. It's been reported that the online shopping empire has been talking to the largest owner of malls in the States, Simon Property Group, about turning vacant department stores into Amazon fulfilment centres. For my part, I'd rather we leave our malls as abandoned hulks—fodder for spooky photographs. A civilization should have to reckon with its losses. Some of us aren't done mourning.

Cloverdale, of course, is doomed. A looming condo development—with a handful of stores quoting Cloverdale's early open-air history—will soon uproot the mall. The proposed concept art sure looks utopian. There are model-train trees, pedestrian paths, and a gesture at a playground. Apparently, the Cloverdale name will persist.

It's all wrong, though. It's not grubby enough. It's not been properly smoked. My late father's brand of pure browsing—ever on the cusp of loitering, with bread for the seagulls—surely won't be tolerated by the condo owners.

Still, I wouldn't necessarily wish my childhood on my own children, even if I do hope they can learn how to be alone with themselves, a skill that seems to have fallen the way of cursive. Perhaps it's strange to mourn the mall—to mourn an institution that helped put paid to many smaller independent shops. (The mall will always be less likeable than main street.) In any case, that childhood—free of Sunday shopping and smartphone alerts—has gone the way of dinosaurs, the dodo, and Sears. Being left to your own devices now means never being bored again.

An Elegy
for Effort,
Memory,
and Passion

IN THE EARLY decades of the twentieth century, a great
civilization of Jewish wits occupied Vienna's coffeehouses.
Some, like the journalist Alfred Polgar, achieved renown;
others, like the romantically unproductive Peter Altenberg, cult status. An anti-Semitic quota system prevented
many of these writers from becoming university faculty;
they were forced to thrive amid clinking cups and noisy
conversation. (Altenberg even had his mail directed to
his preferred haunt, Café Central.) The coming of the
Second World War, however, eventually emptied the coffeehouses. Vienna's Jewish writers were dispersed and, in
some cases, forgotten.

One of the great fans of these now-obscure writers
was the Australian critic Clive James, who absorbed
much of his enthusiasm for the coffeehouse wits from the
pianist Alfred Brendel. As James tells it,

Brendel carries on his person their best sayings, individually typed out on slips of paper. Away from the piano, Brendel's fingertips are usually wrapped in strips of Elastoplast. (So would mine be, if they were worth ten million dollars each.) When you see those bits of paper being hauled from his pockets by his plastered fingers, you realize you are in the presence of a true enthusiast.

It's a memorable anecdote, in part because of Brendel's commitment to remembering, in part because of his monk-like faith in print media. Nowadays, an enthusiast talking up his heroes to an innocent would probably produce a smartphone.

The internet certainly gives the illusion of being a great enabler of enthusiasm. There's no lack of links to email to nonbelievers, no shortage of fan sites or chat rooms in which those who share a very specific fetish can organize. All manner of button lets you share or retweet at will. (No slips of paper need change plastered hands.) Platforms like YouTube permit lay-archivists to post grey literature that would otherwise be inaccessible, like the reclusive Canadian singer Mary Margaret O'Hara's lone Christmas original.

But if it's the perfect time to be an obscure work of art, it's also end-times for Brendel's breed of cult enthusiast; our information-deluged era has rendered his ascetic devotion obsolete. It's not just that the champions of the obscure have been spoiled by the ease with which they can express their fandom; it's that their most important function, keeping a torch lit for the lesser known, has been taken over by the web.

* * *

NOT SO LONG ago, the obsessive fan had no easy way to instantly preserve and share the obscure object of her enthusiasm. The writer with a pet interest pitched it to editors and hoped it landed. The amateur, in possession of no editors' ears, founded fan clubs and mimeographed fanzines. The music aficionado patronized record stores, the bibliophile, estate sales. Bins were combed through, library stacks dragged. Fandom demanded physical effort, and effort ran on passion. Writing about the obscure Canadian poet Charles Bruce, the Montreal-based poet-critic Carmine Starnino notes,

> I certainly had no clue of his existence until my friend Michael Harris picked up *The Mulgrave Road* (for ten cents!) during a Saturday morning visit to a Westmount estate sale. He invited me over to his home that afternoon. He was excited ...

Harris proceeds to read a poem from Bruce's forgotten classic of Canadian poetry: contraband salvaged from the void.

Fandom also required memory—the analogue kind you keep between your ears. The obsessive fan of yesteryear couldn't count on an archive of linked computers, coupled to a search algorithm as intelligent as the one devised by Sergey Brin and Larry Page. Maverick reputations like Weldon Kees (poet), Monte Hellman (filmmaker), Karen Dalton (folky), and Nick Drake (ditto) survived because they were internalized by devotees—as opposed to externalized on YouTube or personal blogs.

For example, the work of the late musician Dennis Wilson was long coveted by an elect group who knew that he was so much more than simply The Beach Boys' reckless also-ran drummer. The only one who'd ever really surfed, Wilson wrote raw, impressionistic songs that Beach Boys albums couldn't quite metabolize. "We didn't know what we had," said bandmate Al Jardine regretfully, decades later. As the band pursued an increasingly kitschy incarnation of itself, Wilson stockpiled his unwanted work: off-brand ballads and rockers that took unexpected turns, his damaged voice riding a widescreen orchestral swell like driftwood.

Some of the songs appeared on Wilson's one solo album, 1977's *Pacific Ocean Blue*, which went out of print for years. (A 1991 CD became a collector's item.) Some of the best songs weren't even released. They had to hole up in the minds of monks. "I heard [the instrumental track] 'Holy Man' only once when we did a rough mix of it in March of 1976," recalls one of Wilson's sound engineers, John Hanlon. "Then it sat in my head for thirty-one years. I couldn't hear it anywhere else. They hadn't done any vocals, but it was such a magical melody that I would've done anything just to hear the track one more time."

To supplement memory, the obsessive fan of yesteryear was forced to covet and seek out used editions, bootlegs, grainy video, hearsay, rumour, word of mouth, brittle clippings, Brendel's slips of paper, cassette tape, and other ephemera. But "forced" suggests his poverty was a bad thing. In fact, lack of content correlates to deeper commitment. The obsessive fan slaked his thirst with droplets of data, spaced out across months, even years. Yes, I know, I sound like a wartime propagandist. But lack of content—an intolerable proposition in the Age of Scrolling, when one post displaces the next by flick of thumb—taught frugality and toughened consumers of culture into cacti. They would've been scandalized by the hyperlinks that geyser out of online essays.

Don't get me wrong; it's lovely to type a name into a search bar and call up content about some little-known figure you care about. A deserving artist or work shouldn't be the preserve of a few. But the dedicated, discerning obsessive understood the irreplaceable value of physical effort, of combing the inhospitable world. If you took Richard Teleky's creative writing classes in the 1990s, you would've felt obliged to look up many neglected but deserving books, including Paula Fox's *Desperate Characters*. A slim, cleanly executed novel that takes place over the course of a weekend, it concerns a Brooklyn couple trying to find a cat. (The wife is bitten at the start of the novel and spends the length of it worried about rabies.)

The book disappeared for years, but then Jonathan Franzen, Fox's most famous fan, campaigned to get it brought back into print. (Kurt Cobain and Courtney Love did something similar in 1993, using newly acquired power to persuade Geffen Records to reissue albums by the neglected English band The Raincoats.) Anyway, during the dark age of *Desperate Characters*, Teleky did his part; he bought up used copies, whenever he stumbled on them in stores, and made them gifts. That was how, in a chilly vacuum without AbeBooks, Teleky attended to his torch-work.

* * *

"25 YEARS AGO I tore this Richard Wilbur poem out of the New Yorker because I loved it so much," began a recent

tweet by the poetry critic Kamran Javadizadeh. Below the
tweet, Javadizadeh had attached a photo of the magazine
page. The page was frayed, only vaguely rectangular, and
deeply wrinkled; fine tributaries of shadow ran through
and rippled the poem's words. What's more, a pair of
rents, in the bottom righthand corner, had partially
obscured Wilbur's name. In short, the page looked like
papyrus torn from a codex by some misfit Benedictine.
But the poem, "For C.," was still there, still singing
behind the wrinkles.

The tweet itself—an ironic home for so tattered a
thing—had drawn over five hundred likes. But the likes
paled in comparison to the love. Javadizadeh, after all,
had kept the page for a quarter of a century. He had
clearly cherished this piece of paper. And the paper, in
turn, had nourished him.

I've held onto a lot of paper over the years. I still have
the first issue of *Poetry* magazine I ever bought—the April
2004 issue—which singlehandedly introduced me to four
poets I would come to adore: Christian Wiman, Kay Ryan,
Samuel Menashe, and A. E. Stallings. I still have a xerox
of an essay by Ryan, which I made at the York University
library, a bound volume of the bygone magazine *Parnas-
sus* splayed flat on the photocopier. I still have the 2005
issue of *Bookforum* that was devoted to Thomas Pynchon.
I still have dozens of issues of *MOJO* magazine, going back
over twenty years. They form stacks on the floor of my
bedroom and occupy bins in my shed. The Al Jardine
quote, above, comes from a *MOJO*—from the very article
that introduced me to Dennis Wilson's work.

Occasionally, I revisit online articles. I do! But sometimes the content goes missing. Sometimes paywalls

drop like the door of a citadel, or a revamped website, blasé about its own past, distorts an article's formatting. Paper is surely the better medium to remember by. It's tactile—it's palpable. Its words are really there, composed of ink. (No battery is required to maintain their shape.) Plus, print is portable. An old number of a magazine can be borne away like a Bible.

It can even *become* your Bible. I spent years tracking down the work of cult artists showcased in the February 2000 issue of *MOJO*. That single edition—with longform features on Big Star, Fred Neil, and The La's—fired my browsing for the better part of two decades. It was the multipage sidebar that transfixed me: dozens of capsule summaries of obscurities like Liam Hayes (a reclusive songwriter from Chicago) and James Booker (once described by Dr. John as "the best black, gay, one-eyed junkie piano genius New Orleans has ever produced").

Obviously, more info about these artists existed *somewhere* in the world. But the internet circa 2000 CE contained exponentially less content than it does today. Hayes and Booker effectively didn't exist outside of *MOJO*. Those capsule summaries were gospels.

* * *

IF ANYTHING, THE hardship that came with seeking out artists like Hayes was part of the pleasure of listening to them. Hayes was the auteur behind a near-mythical Chicago band called Plush. The music of Plush made compact with the carefully arranged work of Brian Wilson, Jimmy Webb, and other soft-pop maestros who have nothing to do with our current zeitgeist. To wit: Plush's

2002 album *Fed* was painstakingly recorded on analogue tape and arranged by the guy who did the strings for Earth, Wind & Fire. (It's a record that wasn't of its time because it was for *all* time.) *Fed* cost so much to make, though, that it struggled to find US distribution. A Japanese label took up the cause, and Chicago's Reckless Records resolved to stock the pricey import, which is how I came by my copy. Listening to *Fed*—a masterpiece that relatively few people knew about in 2002—felt strange, like I was hoarding the only extant copy of a lost Beatles album.

As for Hayes, he remains a figure out of time. The preamble to a 2018 interview describes the songwriter's "extremely offline" life:

> No Twitter account, no Facebook, not even text or emails. You wanna interview Hayes? You gotta know someone who knows someone... type up some interview questions, send them on over and wait for scanned, type-written pages to show up.

Like a Liam Hayes record, the auteur's attention was a hard-won commodity; the obsessive artist demanded obsession from his fans. You couldn't casually enjoy Hayes's work; you were, by default, a diehard. (Even his most recent album, 2018's *Mirage Garage*, came out on cassette initially—a middle finger to our digital moment.) Now, of course, you can easily download Hayes's music to your preferred device.

Perhaps I'm a pair of binoculars away from birding with Franzen. Perhaps we should be happy to see the work of neglected but deserving artists digitized and made widely available. But there's something to lament in the obsolete figure of the obsessive fan, who made the best of his barbarian epoch. We should mourn the monk-like devotees of Wilson, Fox, Hayes, and others, who carried the fragile reputations of their charges this far, far enough to see them uploaded forever—so long as the links don't break.

I Remember the Bookstore

LET'S BROWSE A bookstore—a Platonic one, a composite. Let's wander an aisle, running our fingertips across a wall of spines. One spine, thick and black, juts out: the recent NYRB Classics reissue of William Gaddis's novel *The Recognitions*. It's a block of a book, though you'd never know that, scrolling online. The back cover even features a blurb by Don DeLillo. Let's linger on it.

> I remember the bookstore, long gone now, on Forty-Second Street. I stood in the narrow aisle reading the first paragraph of *The Recognitions*. It was a revelation, a piece of writing with the beauty and texture of a Shakespearean monologue—or, maybe more apt, a work of Renaissance art impossibly transformed from image to words. And they were the words of a contemporary American. This, to me, was the wonder of it.

There's a lot to like about this blurb. There's the spectacle of one great novelist plumping for the work of another.

There's the real-time search for the right words ("or, maybe more apt") and the wonderful ones arrived at ("a work of Renaissance art impossibly transformed from image to words"). There's the subtext of a green writer, a budding DeLillo, stumbling on the kind of writing he hadn't *thought* was native to his American soil, something he didn't even realize he was searching for. "And they were the words of a contemporary American," he tells us, in awe. "This, to me, was the wonder of it." There's a bildungsroman buried in DeLillo's blurb.

But then there's that opening bit, which the blurb could reasonably live without. "I remember the bookstore, long gone now, on Forty-Second Street," writes DeLillo, eating up precious back-cover real estate.

Why recall the bookstore where he first read the opening paragraph of *The Recognitions*? Perhaps the paragraph was so brilliant it imprinted the moment on DeLillo's memory as if on film. Perhaps it was a Proustian madeleine, a prod to memory. Or maybe the bookstore itself played a part in DeLillo's first encounter with *The Recognitions*. Maybe something in the very plaster pulled him to Gaddis's book. Whatever the case, the bookstore had stuck with him. Stuck *to* him. Paragraph and place had fused in the novelist's mind.

* * *

I can certainly remember where I was when I first encountered a great many of my favourite books. I never meant to keep these memories; I seem to have had no say in the matter. The bookstores, my mind decided, were important: the setting for a bildungsroman.

For instance, I remember standing in Toronto's World's Biggest Bookstore—"long gone now," to lift DeLillo's line. It was around 1996, and I was considering a paperback copy of Neal Stephenson's novel *Snow Crash*. The cover, you see, had cried out to my teenage self. A ninja type, sword raised, stands before an arch of ancient brickwork, bulging with duelling bulls in relief. But beyond the arch, across a plain of circuitry, a futuristic skyline awaits. Above the title, a header declares the book to be "THE #1 SCIENCE FICTION BESTSELLER," the definite article doing some work. Below the title, a blurb from something called *Los Angeles Reader* (also "long gone now") is blunt: "Stephenson has not stepped, he has vaulted onto the literary stage with this novel."

On the back cover, there's a vote of confidence from William Gibson no less, maybe my favourite writer, plus other appealing endorsements. "A cross between *Neuromancer* and Thomas Pynchon's *Vineland*," says one blurb. A "gigathriller" sporting a "cool, hip cybersensibility," says the publisher's copy. Hey, it was the 1990s.

I stood there, holding the paperback. The World's Biggest Bookstore was low-ceilinged and harshly lit, with many rows of orange shelves. The building itself had two floors, one entrance, and a long approach, and there was usually a homeless person right by the doors, so you had time to root for change or steel yourself, especially if you were a shy, naive kid from the suburbs. It wasn't as obviously welcoming as the tony megastores of today, like Indigo, which dedicate a lot of space to pillows, candles, and Starbucks (though I seem to recall the World's Biggest, late in its life, grudgingly attempting a café—a counter with a few tables).

Still, you could linger there for hours because of the sheer volume of books. Tongue in cheek, the store marketed itself as an admirably shabby foil to its competitors: "We occasionally have soft mood lighting. But then we replaced the burnt out fluorescent tubes." World's Biggest was about the books, shelves and shelves of them. When my father and I were downtown, we'd often arrange to split up for an hour or so, then meet at the bookstore. If one of us was late, the other would have more than enough to occupy himself with. This was before smartphones, when killing time took creativity.

Anyway, perhaps I looked like I was on the fence, because a passing employee paused long enough to inform me that the book I was holding was excellent. I remember a thin, middle-aged woman with jet-black hair, bearing a stack of books. I want to say she was wearing the sort of apron bookstores foist on their staff, and black shoes, maybe even Doc Martens. She gave off the vibe of a mostly reformed Goth, someone who'd dabbled in dark arts or, at least, Neil Gaiman comics. I immediately decided she was childless, a serious reader, trustworthy, and very cool. I bought the book.

As I grew older and spent more time with friends, I tried to continue the practice of arranging to meet at large bookstores, where the early worm might browse for a bit. But World's Biggest—which was owned by Coles, a chain eventually absorbed by Indigo—was torn down in 2014. You could buy a latte at the newer, upscale stores. You could retreat to a comfy chair or even listen to live music on an actual piano. But standing around under strong lighting—basically loitering as you waited for ex-Goth angels, clad in dark raiment, to descend and offer guidance—was off brand and off the table.

* * *

I'VE NEVER THOUGHT about a book I own and then recalled where I was when I ordered it off a website. Perhaps I was sitting at the dining room table. Perhaps I had my laptop on the sofa. Screens absorb and disperse us. When we're online, we're everywhere—and nowhere.

It could've been otherwise. When William Gibson minted the term "cyberspace" in his 1982 short story "Burning Chrome," he imagined something like an internet, but in *spatial* terms. You "jacked in" using an Ono-Sendai vii deck and a pair of trodes, the trodes held in place by a "white terry sweatband." Here is one of Gibson's characters, a hacker, describing cyberspace:

A silver tide of phosphenes boiled across my field of vision as the matrix began to unfold in my head, a 3-D chessboard, infinite and perfectly transparent. . . . Legitimate programmers jack into their employers' sector of the matrix and find themselves surrounded by bright geometries representing the corporate data.

Gibson's vision of linked computers was prescient, but quaint too. Cyberspace was still a "somewhere," a grid populated with "bright geometries," a terrain to navigate, to move through.

A decade later, in *Snow Crash*, Neal Stephenson refined Gibson's idea and proposed the "Metaverse" (no relation to Mark Zuckerberg's). Accessible via goggles, the Metaverse is organized around the so-called Street, a "grand boulevard going all the way around the equator of a black sphere with a radius of a bit more than ten thousand kilometers. That makes it 65,536 kilometers around, which is considerably bigger than the Earth." You can customize your avatar, but be warned: "cheap public terminals" produce a "jerky, grainy black and white." There are "vast hovering overhead light shows" and "free-combat zones where people can go to hunt and kill each other." You can "write car and motorcycle software" and take your "software out and race it in the black desert of the electronic night." In the Metaverse, the code's the limit.

We didn't get these sci-fi internets, of course. We didn't even get the internet as originally advertised. (The early, buzzy metaphors—"information superhighway," "surfing"—promised dynamic motion.) Instead, we got an endlessly metastasizing stack of two-dimensional pages— and browsers to sort them. But then the language of "browser" is a feint as well. You don't "browse" the internet. You don't move *through* it. It's a galaxy's worth of content with none of the space. It's infinite density. You either already know what you want to see (and duly type in the URL) or you try the search bar, which can bring up millions of possibilities. You can keep many different browsers open at once, fanned out like cards from decks of different provenance, a bespoke set specific to your needs. Miraculous, sure, but you're never quite *somewhere*. There are no aisles, no vistas, no long views.

We've grown used to this atomized, blinkered arrangement, each of us in our carousel, fed by our feed. We've acclimated to online shopping, to typing in the title of a book and being hustled straight away to its unique page. We've given up the journey for the destination. We've achieved two-dimensional teleportation.

There was something steadying, though, about standing in an actual, cavernous bookstore and taking it all in.

Your fellow customers shared a room and a set of options. The scale was human, and the stock was present. Some of it disappeared from day to day as people purchased books. But you had to walk past the stuff you *thought* you didn't want to reach the stuff you thought you *did*. Thus, you could stumble on something you hadn't set out for. (I'd never heard of *Snow Crash* the day I picked it up.)

Or you could cozy up to a title slowly, over time, flirting with the idea of it. I remember visiting a copy of the novel *Gravity's Rainbow*, by Thomas Pynchon, over and over. It resided at The Book Company in Sherway Gardens. I'd won a high school English prize, and my teachers had arranged a gift certificate for the store. Thirty dollars, if I recall. A fortune for a teenager in the 1990s.

There's plenty of information about the World's Biggest Bookstore online, but there are only two hits on the entire internet that remember, by name, The Book Company at Sherway Gardens. The store seems to fall within what writer Tom Scocca calls

> the Internet Event Horizon, the gap between those things that were around to be incorporated in real time into the eternal present of the World Wide Web, and those pre-Web things that were old enough that the World Wide Web reached back and made note of them for their nostalgia value.

The first hit, a blog post, features a digitized Polaroid snapped at a 1990 Douglas Adams book signing. The blog's text describes the store as "a lavish, decadent shrine to literature, swathed in dark, classy forest green"—a shade purple, that, but it confirms my memories. The second hit, on Reddit, is about the exact same signing and references "a now-extinct bookstore in Sherway Gardens, The Book Company." Worryingly, both blog and Reddit post are by the same author. Are we the only two who remember? (It turns out there were a few other Book Companies, including one in Ottawa which the Indigo Empire gobbled up and eventually shuttered.)

In any case, my teenage self had judged The Book Company in "dark, classy forest green" a serious store, and *Gravity's Rainbow* a serious novel. I'd been eyeing it for some time, the Penguin Twentieth-Century Classics edition, with mint green spine, V2 rocket blueprints for a cover, and that iconic Christopher Lehmann-Haupt quote on the back, which might've invented the very idea of desert islands:

> Fantastic! ... Fantastically large, complex, funny, perplexing, daring, and weird ... If I were banished to the moon tomorrow and could take only five books along, this would have to be one of them.

"Weird," indeed; the plot summary described a book whose main character's "sexual conquests" are correlated to "V-2 rocket bombs ... falling on London ..." Clearly, *Gravity's Rainbow* was a classic of some kind, but kooky too. Contraband hiding in plain sight. Words for a high school student to get high on.

I'd been circling the book for some time. (I'd also been circling the Penguin Twentieth-Century Classics *Ulysses*, with the cover shot of James Joyce in Shakespeare and Company, the Paris bookstore that published the novel's first edition.) The *Gravity's Rainbow* was in mint condition—except for a small white crease in the upper right-hand corner of its cover. Sign of in-store manhandling? Minor mishap at the printer? I was fussy about my books, and the crease had been bothering me, which is why I'd been reluctant to close the deal. The crease was a barrier to cross.

Nearly twenty-five years later, the book is still with me. It's yellowed some, and the corners have lost their crisp points. The spine stayed smooth (I never crack a spine if I can help it), but I worry about the cover, which is beginning to show signs of detaching. The crease is still there, of course, a little creek I've learned to live alongside. Surely every *Gravity's Rainbow* should have one.

* * *

A FEW YEARS later, I was browsing in Pages, an independent bookstore in downtown Toronto. By this time, my passion had passed from fiction to poetry. And yet I'd struggled to admire Canadian poetry or, rather, the attenuated version my profs had been pushing in university. A species of free verse bordering on plain speech, Canadian poetry waved off the metaphor and music—too florid. Instead, it counted itself direct and unshowy. It even seemed to take perverse pride in its lack of vision. "The animals / have the faces of / animals," says one Margaret Atwood poem, coolly, as if avoiding description were a positive; as if conjuring a blank in the reader's mind were an act of courage. Canadian poetry was as scrubbed of formal texture as a prairie.

But there seemed to be an embargo on saying as much. Canadian poetry was a duty read. A pity read. It demanded

patriotism and kid gloves. Book stores gave the frail stuff
its own shelf, isolated from the other poetry. Anthologies
like Gary Geddes's *15 Canadian Poets x 2* kept Canadian
poetry on life-support. Homegrown garlands, like the
Governor General's Award, were gently placed.

All of this I understood half-consciously, somewhere in
my gut, where the acidic feelings churn. But a military-ed-
ucational complex had arisen around the work of Atwood,
Al Purdy, Michael Ondaatje, Anne Carson, and so many
other officially approved mediocrities. A campaign of bad
opinions—reinforced by journalists, prize committees,
and academics—can buffet one's confidence. You can
start to second-guess yourself. It's not the poems, it's you.

It was in this mental climate that I lifted Carmine
Starnino's book of essays *A Lover's Quarrel* off the new
releases table at Pages, leafed through it, and felt a crackle
of kinship. Here are the first few sentences:

> I want to do this right, and the best way to begin is
> to fess up to reservations. Luckily, I have a few.
> Chief among them is whether these previously pub-
> lished reviews, stacked a decade deep, are
> interesting enough to survive the second life I've
> forced upon them. Such resurrectionist strivings
> have always seemed suspect to me. Past its occasion,
> a review's relevance isn't likely to run very high,
> and it's a rare opinion that, appearing imperishably
> robust on first print, doesn't evaporate into vapidity
> when invited back for a permanent stay between
> covers. I can only hope that's not the case here. I've
> also been put on notice by the fanaticism with
> which others have fattened similar collections.

It was the style that struck me—the image of "published reviews, stacked a decade deep," the barely concealed rhyme in "evaporate into vapidity," the wicked alliteration of "fanaticism" and "fattened."

I hadn't been looking for *A Lover's Quarrel* that day—I hadn't even known it existed. But Pages had armed me with an IED of a book. Here was a critic exploding pieties and expressing the very doubts I'd long kept contained in my mind. Here was a critic dragging Canada's past for the worthy poets we'd cast off, the poets whose work hadn't fit our narrow definition of Canadian poetry. Surely someone had erred in placing Starnino's subversive book in plain view.

That was the joy of an indie like Pages; it stacked the Starninos on the sort of precious prominent real estate a larger chain reserves for the bestsellers that need no help finding readers' hands. That is, Pages stacked the deck in favour of the quirky, the prickly, the heroically uncommercial. In favour of *discovery*. *A Lover's Quarrel* never shifted *that* many units; it was never going to be a Heather's Pick. But its dissident sensibilities riled and reshaped a generation of poets and critics.

Sadly, Pages vanished a few years later, in 2009, a victim of Toronto's swelling rents. But Starnino's book had left its blast crater.

* * *

IMAGINE A VERSION of the contemporary web laid out before us, like Gibson's cyberspace or Stephenson's Metaverse. Picture an endless plateau, planed flat, with aloof skyscrapers: a gleaming city in draft, a Dubai dispersed. That giant TV on the horizon is YouTube, that tower of shipping boxes, Amazon. Smaller structures suggest modest websites: businesses, blogs, and more. The buildings roll away, as regular as dominoes, around the horizon. Occasional fissures, venting steam, allude to the catacombs of the dark web.

In this vision, your browser is a pod. You punch in coordinates and zip around at light-speed, passing smoothly through other browsers, whose hulls turn transparent at your approach, as in the Metaverse. Hyperlinks are wormholes: tunnels of swirling light.

One wormhole wings your pod across a digital Atlantic and deposits you in front of a quaint green building on the banks of a pixelated river. Other quaint buildings surround it but are spaced apart to accommodate pods. (It's as if someone clicked on the edge of a city and dragged it, distending space itself.) You are now at the online shop for Shakespeare and Company, on the banks of the Seine in Paris. It's never closed, and the door is decoration: you float cleanly through it.

Inside, your pod hangs like a wasp, scanning spines. You move down the centre of aisles like a steady cam shot in Kubrick. You alight on the roof of a stack of books, rising from the new releases table. The store senses that you're squinting at something—the new Sally Rooney. The cover sharpens. Text boxes bloom in midair—blurbs, hot takes, a JPEG of the Irish author, a throbbing BUY NOW button. You look away, and the book dims, the boxes closing like tulips.

Time travel is an option here. You toggle to a 1922 version of the store, managed by the long-gone Sylvia Beach, and scrutinize a first edition of *Ulysses*, with blue cover, the one James Joyce's first reviewers likened to a phonebook. In microseconds, Shakespeare and Company's invisible AI, lurking on some server, has worked up a précis on the available copies, including prices and comps from recent auctions.

Perhaps this is what browsing bookstores will be like in the future. Still, I'd give up my vision of aerodynamic pods and virtual aisles for a few more afternoons among the grubby orange shelves of the World's Biggest Bookstore.

* * *

I'VE BOUGHT PLENTY of books online, books that have come to mean something to me. But location matters to our minds. We all have personal associations—individual, inner text boxes—which float above certain objects. They can't be swatted away. "I remember the bookstore," begins Don DeLillo. He will never forget it.

Writing this essay, I was surprised to find myself growing emotional. Google's supply of images of the World's Biggest Bookstore conjured a lost civilization and its peoples, including memories of teachers I adored, my late father, and other ghosts. What had I been doing while the civilization crumbled? I'd been busy, I suppose—with grad school, a failed marriage, career, a new marriage, kids, poems, essays. By 2021, many of the bricks-and-mortar bookstores I'd browsed in my youth were gone.

But some, like Bakka-Phoenix Books (an indie specializing in sci-fi and fantasy) and Book City (an indie chain), survived. Plus, new shoots *have* sprung up: Ben McNally Books in 2007, Queen Books in 2017, a Type Books here and there. The stores tend to be in high-density, gentrified, and walkable neighbourhoods. (The suburb I grew up in will likely never draw a Type, with its trendy totes, to the local plaza.) And the new stores aren't as desirably dingy as, say, Pages. I'm glad they exist, though. They're offering sanctuary and succor to the next generation.

Consider Ben McNally Books, which started out in Toronto's financial district, in the sort of high-ceilinged, chandeliered, and ornately columned space once reserved for banks. (It has since decamped east.) Ben McNally offers a thoroughly grownup browsing experience, with beautiful wooden shelves, excellent non-fiction and poetry sections, and book launches. (It has even launched yours truly.)

But the shop's most valuable contribution is its calm, authoritative curation. I recall the Ben McNally shelf dedicated to the NYRB Classics imprint—the very same imprint that revived *The Recognitions*. (NYRB Classics is to literature what the Criterion Collection is to film: a prestige label addressed to connoisseurs.) What a delight to discover a bookstore that had corralled the imprint's individual titles in one section. (What an innovation: curation by publisher!) Different but brilliant books that demand discovery—like Arthur Schnitzler's *Late Fame* and Patrick Leigh Fermor's *A Time of Gifts*—always make more sense grouped together. A well-curated indie like Ben McNally helps you make those connections. It hyperlinks its wares the old-fashioned way.

Or consider the new bookstore in the east end of my city, the Scribe. Defiantly launched during the pandemic by Justin Daniel Wood, the Scribe is a vintage concern devoted to the exquisitely old: to first editions, signed books, and antiquarian delights. What I've most enjoyed, though, is turning up affordable books that have gotten harder to source in bricks-and-mortar shops, like, say, Bruce Sterling's *Heavy Weather*, a 1994 sci-fi novel about tornado chasers (which I remember first spotting at World's Biggest). The first edition I picked up at the Scribe happens to be signed, but I was happy just to have found a reading copy.

You can't scroll through a formal catalogue, but the Scribe updates online photos of its shelves every week so that, in the words of its website, "you can browse from your living room couch." But there's no substitute for standing on the Scribe's antique hardwood floor and hefting a beautifully preserved, out-of-print book in your hand. Plus, you can't always believe your eyes when scrolling—someone might've already borne away the book you're eyeballing—but you can believe them when browsing. The real world never struggles to load content. The real world never freezes.

Whether you choose to visit the Scribe in vintage flesh or shelter at home and squint at pixelated spines, Wood's store is selling something special: a product we want precisely *because* it occupies space, because it came from a printing press and survived its early handlers. It's a relief, really, to encounter something that doesn't have a digital doppelgänger—a digital solution. The point is the paper, the poignantly musty smell of the past. E-books and NFTs have yet to figure out how to yellow handsomely with age.

Still, Toronto's renaissance aside, it's hard not to miss the specific stores that once offered my young self sanctuary and succor. They weren't just stores, after all; they were hothouses that helped me grow into a reader and

writer. How often the aisles, back then, steered my aimless mind. How often I simply stood around, still, as if I
were potted, thumbing through a book I knew nothing
about. Sometimes I was waiting for someone, sometimes
I was on my own. But there was no way for anyone to
reach me. How wonderfully subversive it was to feel like
I was alone in a city. No alerts, no pop-ups. Just the press
of books all around, the world distilled to words on a page.

* * *

THERE'S A POSTSCRIPT to the *Snow Crash* story. Not long
after buying it, I loaned it to a high school classmate. The
book came back a mess: cover scuffed, spine cracked,
edges blunted. The classmate wasn't a fetishist—just a
reader. My (eternal) bad: handing the book over, I had
failed to convey my fussiness.

The book stayed with me, but the state of it needled. So,
a few years ago, I decided I'd try to source a new copy of
the same nineties-era edition. A mint copy to supplement
the mangled one. *Snow Crash* had since wriggled into and
out of several cover designs, but I didn't want any of them.
I wanted the one commended to me by the ex-Goth angel.

I tried different websites. None was very promising.
You could certainly find a copy, but I couldn't seem to
secure a mint specimen, and anyway, I didn't trust these
faceless sellers' descriptions of the state of their stock.
This was a mass-market paperback from over twenty
years ago. How many decent copies had even made it into
the twenty-first century?

Reader, after many months of searching, having abandoned the internet, while browsing She Said Boom!

(exclamation point theirs), a used book and record store in Toronto, browsing in the flesh, alone, just before the pandemic—I found my out-of-print *Snow Crash*. Not only was it in pristine condition, but it also seemed to have been opened exactly once when its original owner had slipped the receipt in the inside cover. I know this because the receipt was still there; it had left a rectangle of white on the browned cardstock, indicating where it had turned back the slow creep of light and air.

The receipt was dated 1995. Printed at the top, in ink that had dried a quarter of a century ago, were the words "World's Biggest Bookstore."

Second Spin

A FEW YEARS ago, the 1980s band Felt began reissuing its early, out-of-print albums. Each one comes in a box with a remastered CD and a seven-inch vinyl single. Each dangles assorted lures like buttons and a poster. They're not cheap; at $50 a pop, these reissues are basically bait for nostalgic grownups with an income.

But when I went on Amazon to source a cheaper version of the band's first two albums—a twofer CD I'd owned and sold in grad school—I discovered the disc was going for more than $1,200. I refreshed the browser. Twelve hundred dollars.

Many things once thought worthless—vinyl records, Brutalism—have grown in value. The internet, which leaves no take unturned, has been predicting a compact disc comeback for years. After seeing what my lost Felt CD was now selling for, I began checking the prices of the CDs I'd held onto. A solo album by Kevin Rowland, of Dexys Midnight Runners, turns out to be worth $100 to $200 on Amazon. A couple Alex Chilton discs fall within the same price range. I was pleased but scandalized too; I'd been so negligent with this treasure.

My CD collection had fallen into disrepair. I'd never completely kicked the habit of buying compact discs. They're cheap, after all, and still accepted into iTunes. (I haven't updated our MacBook with whatever came after.) But from time to time, as a cash-strapped PhD candidate, I had to carve out and liquidate parcels of my collection. The survivors followed me through several moves and acquired scratches. Cracks inched across their jewel cases. (A beloved box of Oasis singles, which quoted Benson & Hedges packaging, fell, and shattered at the hinge.) My CDs lost their dedicated housing—those bygone towers with the horizontal slots—and wound up on shelving, bunkered in my basement. They were no longer even alphabetized.

In David Cronenberg's film *Videodrome*, a media scholar named Professor Brian O'Blivion, modeled after Marshall McLuhan, has created an archive of videocassettes. There seems to be a cassette for every occasion; each contains a recording of O'Blivion holding forth. The collection, in other words, is his cloud. He has backed up his soul.

Reflecting on the ruins of my own maimed, semi-dispersed, and not entirely worthless collection of physical media, I realized that some small part of myself that I'd externalized—which I'd made material—had been abandoned. Betrayed.

* * *

I'M A LATE adopter. Long after the world had embraced the Discman, I still preferred my Walkman. I liked that I couldn't fast forward past subpar songs without draining the battery; I had to endure whole albums, one side at a time. Plus, the subpar songs sharpened my love for the better ones. They were the vegetables, deployed to delay and draw out the better bites. Not that there were many of them; I'd inherited my older sister's cassettes, which furnished a respectable, readymade canon: U2, The Smiths, The Cure, The Jesus and Mary Chain, New Order.

By the time the world had moved on to MP3 players, I was proudly walking around with a silver Discman, cupped like a clutch. It couldn't carry more than one disc at a time, so I couldn't suddenly swap out the album I'd chosen unless I'd thought ahead and packed a bag. In time, I grudgingly allowed an iPod into my life. Still, the thought of shuffling songs, as if they were cards in a board game, seemed cavalier.

I kept buying CDs. I moved them onto my laptop and then onto the iPod. Cords had to be located, hardware plugged in. I told myself I liked limits and wasn't simply romanticizing an aversion to change. Also, the compact disc was *matter*. It could be collected. It came with liner notes, slim booklets on high-end stationery, which smelled good when you took the shrink-wrap off. And the disc itself wasn't without charm. It boiled vinyl down to its Platonic parts: circle and gleam. It made a delicate claw of your hand—a setting for a stone—as you gripped its edges and placed it in its tray.

Eventually, grad school exacted a toll. I didn't have a lot in the bank, but I could withdraw capital from the CDs I no longer loved. And for a time, there were a lot of them; they tempted like a trust fund. The aforementioned Felt CD would've vanished in one of my purges. It was a splendid item. It had a grey and defiantly anti-aesthetic cover, which promoted the bar code and the record label's physical address, details both useless and glorious.

For a time, Second Spin, a small shop in Toronto, paid very well for used CDs. The clerk didn't simply quote an overall figure; he divided up your offering into distinct stacks. Seven bucks for each disc in this stack. Ten for each one here. Your collection was treated with knowledge and respect. With care.

Vortex Records was another favourite destination. It had moved around a few times before finally settling at Yonge and Eglinton. I discovered the store near the end of its four-decade run. The owner—a thin older man named Bert Myers—would make a point of noting tartly when I *bought* a CD or two; I offloaded much more than I ever purchased. I never quite got to know him, but I gathered he was an institution, and that he was seeing, in his waning years, more sellers than buyers. Vortex closed in early 2016.

How did I decide which to keep and which to sell? I suppose I was betting on futures. I sold discs by worthy bands I wasn't actively into, and which I wagered could be replaced later with relative ease (The Beatles). I rid myself of music gone bad, by trendy, invasive bands that had crept onto my radar (The Vines). I dispensed with brief enthusiasms (Vangelis's soundtrack for *Blade Runner*) and signifiers of adolescence (*The Wall*). And I cast out obscurities, like Felt, that had failed to hold my fickle attention.

Still, some mix of sentiment and principle saved certain CDs I had no immediate use for. I could never quite give up my Fred Neil albums. Neil was the author of "Everybody's Talkin'," famously covered by Harry Nilsson in *Midnight Cowboy* (though Neil's version, lacquered in his lovely baritone, is the one to hear). Neil had stopped recording decades ago and was the definition of a cult artist. Amassing his few albums hadn't been easy. The imperial thumb stayed up.

God knows what that liquidated Felt CD subsidized, though. Something unworthy, to be sure. If not a lesser album, then a forgotten meal. Drinks with long-gone friends. Nights I barely recollect.

* * *

TOM SCOCCA HAS a charming essay, about test-driving a Cadillac, called "The Identities We Construct through and around Our Consumption of Commercial Products Are Tissue-Thin and Contingent." That wordy title, which David Foster Wallace would've approved of, is probably true.

Still, it's hard not to feel that a collection, organized by a self, can express something substantial about that self, something beyond "I have cool, eclectic taste." My late father bought and hoarded stamps. He drew intricate grids on 8.5-by-11-inch sheets of paper, in which he positioned his treasures. There are binders and binders of these sheets. Dealers at stamp and coin conventions were awestruck at how he'd chosen to organize his collection. Some "tissue-thin" part of him—his artfulness, his attention to detail—remains entangled in those grids of stamps.

Doesn't a collection, like a life, require care? Don't its constituent parts—whether discs or stamps or Christmas villages—have genealogies that attach to certain people or places? And at a certain point, isn't winnowing a kind of airbrushing? I realize only now that in breaking up my CDs, I was banishing whole phases of my personal history— Britpop, jazz, garage rock, Patti Smith—to oblivion.

A CD stores more than music; it stores memories. I might not remember those nights subsidized by liquidated discs, but when I glance at specific albums, I remember where I got them or who gave them to me. I remember where I was the first time they murmured through my earbuds.

For instance, when I glance at the jewel case for 2004's *Elvis at Sun*, I find myself walking home from my sister's house, as I often did back in the aughts . . .

She had given me my first iPod, see. But my parents' bungalow—where I still lived, a few blocks away—had a dial-up connection. Too slow. So, whenever I bought new CDs, I would head to my sister's. The Wi-Fi was plentiful, and the computer had iTunes. There, I would transfer disc to iPod.

One night, walking home from my sister's, I listened to *Elvis at Sun*, a remaster of the King's first recordings, by feted audio restorer Kevan Budd. It was dark, the street was lined with trees, and "Blue Moon" had never sounded better, more spectral, as I passed beneath the leaves and through the pools of light the street lamps made, shadows slipping all around me like shades.

It was a mild hassle, lugging CDs to my sister's. But it was a religious experience, walking home with Elvis's unvarnished voice between my ears.

* * *

THE MILD HASSLE could be quite fun, actually. Streaming will never replicate the physical rush of scrounging loonies, toonies, quarters, and dimes; throwing a leg over your mountain bike; pedalling several kilometres (sans helmet) to the Sam the Record Man that held on for a time near Toronto's High Park; emptying your coins on the counter; and buying the new Oasis single, "D'You Know What I Mean?" on Compact Disc in 1997 CE.

* * *

AFTER I LEFT grad school and got a job, I no longer had to sell CDs. I held on to my remaining discs because I needed some way of listening to music and modern life doesn't offer acceptable alternatives. YouTube is a trickster realm through which tumble, like space debris, inferior versions of dubious provenance (not to mention fan-made slideshows, as well-meaning as the macaroni art my toddler brings home). Streaming, like renting, makes no long-term sense. Vinyl, at this point, is out of the question, and anyway I need a portable solution. The cloud seems about as trustworthy as real-world cumuli, which have a tendency to vanish. (To wit: *Slate* has reported on the danger of one's prized digital files being gessoed over at the whim of Apple.)

I'm stuck with uploading out-of-print CDs to my discontinued iPod Nano. I refuse to use my phone; I worry I'll shorten its life.

* * *

EVENTUALLY—SADLY—I FOUND MORE reasonable listings for some of the CDs I thought were priceless. (Discogs puts them in the $40-to-$50 range.) Perhaps the predators on Amazon, who've inflated prices, are fishing for more desperate and well-heeled nostalgics than me?

It doesn't matter. The neighbourhood street sale has become a favourite destination. Most of the CDs on offer are worthless, the de rigueur contents of bourgeois basements emptied streetward: Buena Vista Social Club, Bette Midler, Coldplay. But I've encountered several serious collectors, standing with their mixed feelings in front of boxes, CD spines exposed to the sky. *Marquee Moon* by Television. *Compact Disc* by PiL. All for a buck or two. All in great condition. The retired—reformed?—collectors comment on the ones I pull out. They've elected to stream, they tell me, or need the shelf space. I sense my intensity, as I rifle through their prized possessions, is a comfort. A partner hovers near, perhaps to ensure that CDs are, in fact, liquidated. I must seem like an easy mark, carting away stacks of obsolete media; I'm convinced I'm the one perpetrating the con—or rebalancing the universe. At one recent sale, I bought a copy of *H.M.S. Fable* by Shack, which I already own, on principle. It's out of print and went for a dollar.

In fact, I'm buying and alphabetizing compact discs again. I've even ordered a few out-of-print discs, including a used copy of *Back in Denim*. ("Plays mint. Very clean.") Felt's frontman, the surnameless Lawrence, released this obscure album in 1992 under the Denim moniker. It anticipated all the Britpop albums I'd loved and lost. I've seen it going for hundreds but managed to pick it up for about $20. I have no plans to sell it, though; I'd just like to give the disc a good home.

And I finally put up the wall-mounted MUJI CD player, which my wife gave me a few years ago. It's as elegant an object as any turntable. You tug the power cord, which dangles like a tail, to turn it on. The CD isn't glassed in, and spins freely. I keep worrying it'll fly off and embed itself in the ceiling or a scalp. But my discs now enjoy a life outside of both iTunes and the basement, revolving on our kitchen wall while we cook. My son finds the blur mesmerizing.

Three Elegies for Bricks and Mortar

Sam the Record Man

ONLINE SHOPPING PROMISES a painless, lightspeed experience. What's more, it pretends to relegate all labour to your mind and fingers. You scroll, you click, and presto: a package is en route. You don't have to reckon with the conditions of the fulfilment centre through which your package passes. You don't have to look the workers in the eye. A few gears, in an unfathomably vast machine, have briefly meshed on your behalf. A few days later, a package arrives innocently, like a pellet.

But you still must wait a few days. This makes no sense to me! All that global, groaning infrastructure—all that exploitation and dehumanization—to deliver something you used to be able to secure on your own, same day, in person? Perhaps people like getting boxes in the mail.

Perhaps the drones will address this, fetching us our purchases within a matter of hours.

When I wanted something right away, I used to go to Sam the Record Man. Launched as a standalone in 1959, Sam the Record Man was a terrific music and movie chain that once spanned my country. There were 140 Sams; the most iconic one, the flagship store, sat in downtown Toronto, in walking distance of the World's Biggest Bookstore and the HMV Superstore. Its face bore two giant neon records. When people wax nostalgic about Sam the Record Man, they mean this one.

Sam had several floors, a few large rooms, and a warren of smaller spaces. You entered through the south set of doors and exited through the north set, where the cash was located. The tiles underfoot mated to form a scuffed red-and-white chessboard. The walls were red, the bins dingy, but not terribly so. Beyond the giant neon records, Sam didn't bother with frills. It didn't have to; it had all the records and movies you could want.

To wit: sometime at the turn of the century, having pored over the February 2000 MOJO magazine, the issue devoted to cult artists, I decided I needed to hear a Fred Neil CD. Neil was a legend, a folk singer's folk singer. (No less than Bob Dylan got his start playing harp for Neil.) Neil had an uncommonly deep baritone—and the songs to pour into it, classics that included "The Dolphins" and "Everybody's Talkin'." But Neil had been restless. He'd shrugged off recording and touring. He'd managed only a few albums in the 1960s, then slowly receded from music, eventually winding up in Florida. Harry Nilsson's cover of "Everybody's Talkin'," featured in *Midnight Cowboy*, had been a huge hit; it had financed Neil's retirement.

Still, it was the Nilsson *cover* people knew; by the time I'd gotten around to reading about him, Neil himself had faded from the culture. He'd become a cult concern. Even the available double CD—an anthology called *The Many Sides of Fred Neil*, which included the bulk of his work—had been relegated to EMI-Capitol's Special Markets label. It would be hard to find at most stores. Impossible to find in the suburbs.

No matter: I made the twelve-minute walk to Kipling subway, the farthest stop west in Toronto, and headed downtown. There, on the second floor of Sam, in the section of the warren devoted to folk music, I found my copy of *The Many Sides of Fred Neil*. I hadn't phoned ahead to check if it was there. I didn't need to.

You could do that in the Age of Browsing. You could simply set out for the city, show up at a reliable institution like Sam the Record Man, and secure the exotic item you were after. Stores could be trusted to keep a comprehensive stock on hand. You didn't need a fulfilment centre; the world itself, the one you navigated on your feet, was fulfilling enough.

(And yes, I know, I've conscripted a privileged pronoun to browse my mental Sam: a second-person pronoun with a subway pass. After all, "you" had to dwell in or near the metropolis to enjoy its riches.)

You weren't always lucky, of course. But disappointment often led to discovery. These days, a scroller has their browser; they need never be disappointed. (If a desired object is out of stock on one website, the scroller can likely find it somewhere else.) Back then, though, you *were* the browser—a body that had made the trip downtown, a body confronted with shelves and bins. Serendipity, the god of browsing, would see that you went home with something.

Sam always had something. An authoritative intelligence lurked behind its front-faced selections. Unlike algorithms, Sam's carbon-based clerks didn't necessarily care about your preferences, because they knew what was good for you. Even the shelves you had to pass to get to the cash—where, in most stores, the impulse buys lie in wait—were carefully curated. Discounted albums by The Stooges, an acquired taste, presented as you slowly shuffled by. It was as if a grocery store had stocked pickled herring at the checkout lane.

Anyway, most of the time Sam came through. When I required Patti Smith's *Horses* or Plush's *More You Becomes You*, the album was there, in the appropriate CD bin. A tall, cumbersome plastic shell—an anti-theft device—entombed each jewel case and made browsing the bins easy, a matter of rapid clacking.

The empire went bankrupt in 2001, and the flagship store closed in 2007. The land went to Ryerson University, which put up a new building. Just down the street, Yonge-Dundas Square—Toronto's attempt at a Times Square—displays the original neon discs like corpses at a wake.

Meanwhile, a lone Sam the Record Man persists at a mall in Belleville, Ontario. We stop there whenever we drive to Ottawa to visit the in-laws. It's a small, charming simulacrum, and dense with stuff, like its ancestors. You can even buy a T-shirt there that says, "Yes, this is the last Sam the Record Man."

Soundscapes

SOUNDSCAPES WAS A monastery for snobs, located in Toronto's Little Italy. It was a small music store, but tastefully appointed, with shelves of light wood. The sign itself was a stylish riposte to Sam the Record Man–style neon: raised letters followed by an abstracted record (one circle containing a smaller one) in negative relief. Greg Davis, the owner, launched the store in 1999. It lasted for two decades, closing in 2021. Streaming platforms had taken a toll. The pandemic delivered a sharp, tidy blow to the nape.

It's tempting to view the fall of Soundscapes as symbolic of greater decline—in canons, authority, and aesthetics. A few years after the launch of Soundscapes, the "poptimism" bubble was already beginning to unfold and inflate. The "poptimists" were music critics who rejected snobbery and dared to take tacky pop stars like Celine Dion seriously. They were anti-connoisseurs. Contrarians. They had a frothy name, the poptimists, but turned out to be no fun. Like dour revolutionaries the world over, they didn't want to topple a hierarchy; they simply wanted to install a new one. Bob Dylan was out, Taylor Swift in.

"Click culture creates a closed system in which popular acts get more coverage, thus becoming more popular, thus getting more coverage," wrote Saul Austerlitz in the *New York Times* in 2014. The poptimist movement, he suggested, was in tune with the tech and the times. Michael Hann, the former music editor for the *Guardian*, echoed the thought a few years later. "Poptimism's victory was sealed by the rise of algorithms and analytics," observed

Hann. He had felt firsthand the pressure to inflate the worth of worthless music. "You need to be able to justify your coverage, and that meant thinkpieces hailing the cultural significance of the new pop stars. After all, if your publication is serious, and covers subjects because they matter, you have to prove those subjects matter."

The staff at Soundscapes knew what really mattered. When you entered the store and turned right, you encountered a wall of canonical texts like Neil Young's *Tonight's the Night* (a funereal, off-key paean to a fallen roadie and bandmate) or The Smiths' *The Queen Is Dead* (a witty tract on the state of Thatcher-era England). To the left of that wall were a couple modest shelves devoted to new releases. Beyond that, the store had little patience for pop or novelty.

Music shops (the big ones, now extinct) tended to reserve their most visible, vertical real estate for new releases bought in bulk—for Adele, basically. Not Soundscapes. The first time I toured the store, I discovered two curiosities, faced out on a wall display: *Third/Sister Lovers*, the lost album by power pop artisans Big Star, and *Like Flies on Sherbert*, the obscure solo debut by Big Star's lead singer Alex Chilton. These CDs weren't fresh rereleases; in fact, there was no timely reason to display them at all. They were defiantly, hopelessly, untimely. Uncommercial. And yet there they sat, innocently, as if they *deserved* pride of place.

In a better world, uncommercial works of art would always occupy the wall. For a brief time, Soundscapes pretended that world was possible. But they weren't snobby about it—and they weren't averse to pleasure. One time, I brought a copy of *Too-Rye-Ay* by Dexys

Midnight Runners up to the cash, and the clerk smiled
warmly at my choice. Who could argue with the band
behind the smash hit "Come On Eileen"?

Another time, I was looking for a solo album by Hal
Blaine, one of the main drummers in the so-called Wrecking Crew. The Wrecking Crew was an informal collective
of LA session musicians in the 1960s: go-to professionals
who played on everything from The Ronettes' "Be My
Baby" to The Beach Boys' *Pet Sounds*. The Soundscapes
clerk gently suggested that I didn't want to bother with
the solo forays of the individual members of the Wrecking Crew. Better to buy the albums of *other* artists, whom
the Wrecking Crew played behind—and made great. So,
I followed the clerk to a shelf. He produced a compilation
of orchestral jazz-rock by David Axelrod and put it in my
hand. Axelrod's compositions didn't feature Blaine, but
they did boast Earl Palmer, Carol Kaye, and Don Randi—
one of the most thrilling rhythm sections ever assembled
(and sampled by hip hop artists decades later). I still play
that CD to this day. I play it when I don't know what else
to play.

The algorithm that suggests stuff "you might also like"
provides a service that's like the one provided by the carbon-based clerks—but the algorithm doesn't operate
from a place of affection. Spotify's AI takes a so-called
exploit and explore approach: it scrutinizes an individual
user's activities while analyzing what hundreds of millions of others are up to. It contemplates age, gender,
location, and more. (Apparently, taste is tied to geogra-
phy!) The AI takes note of the amount of time a user
spends on certain songs and even eyeballs the user's
doings on social media.

Netflix, for its part, sorts subscribers, based on their activity, into several thousand "taste groups." None of the new-fangled algorithms have feelings about what they foist on us. They could just as easily be analyzing our chess strategies or feeding us conspiracy theories on behalf of a foreign government.

The slightly older Soundscapes clerk, with silver hair, had a particularly gentle and kind affect. He'd comment on the odd item you brought to the cash, offering some encouraging words about your choice. He always seemed to be wearing a paisley dress shirt and gave off the impression of having once owned equity in a punk or mod band. I never learned his name, but he surfaced in the media stories about the end of Soundscapes as one Phil Liberbaum. "I think Soundscapes has been a kind of a cultural centre, not just a retail operation," he told the CBC. "I think it's been a magical place." Liberbaum, a voice-over actor, had been with Soundscapes for seventeen years. Before that, he'd been a well-known DJ in Montreal.

Liberbaum was right—Soundscapes was a "kind of cultural centre." Bands squeezed their gear inside, from time to time, and delivered gigs. You could acquire concert tickets there too. Whenever my friend Evan Jones, a poet and critic based in Manchester, was visiting Toronto, we arranged to meet at Soundscapes. We once ran into each other there, unplanned. Where will we go now?

Soundscapes lost some of that "magic" in the store's waning years. In a bid to court aficionados, it relinquished some of its space to vinyl. The deep selection of CDs suffered. I remember looking for the debut album by the UK punk band The Adverts. The duty clerk furrowed his brow; his computer indicated the CD *was* in the store,

even though neither of us could find it. After a few minutes, he located the disc in the basement, already packed
up in a box ready to be shipped back to the distributor. I
saved it from its fate.

Soundscapes itself couldn't be saved. But its website is
still up. For now, anyway, you can read the farewell
message:

> We'd like to thank all of our loyal customers over the
> years, you have made it all worthwhile! The last 20
> years have seen a golden age in access to the world's
> recorded music history both in physical media and
> online. We were happy to be a part of sharing our
> knowledge of some of that great music with you.
> We hope you enjoyed most of what we sold & rec-
> ommended to you over the years and hope you will
> continue to seek out the music that matters.

Soundscapes was a bastion for unpopular, anti-poptimist
beliefs—that some cultural products "matter" more than
others, that critical expertise ("sharing our knowledge")
counts. I liked standing in the store with a coffee. It was
clean, carefully organized, and humane. Humanist. A
business, sure, but a labour of love as well. We are still
waiting for the algorithms to learn how to love.

Vintage Video

ORSON WELLES'S *CHIMES at Midnight* is an ingenious
mash-up of several of Shakespeare's history plays, includ-

ing *Henry IV, Parts 1 and 2*. Welles plays Falstaff, the rotund, sack-swigging ne'er-do-well, who doubles as a surrogate father for Prince Hal. Hal has been slumming with Falstaff's band of amiable thieves but will soon ascend to the throne and rebuke Falstaff, dashing the old thief's heart on the throne room's floor.

It's considered by many to be Welles's best work—even better than *Citizen Kane*, which is routinely voted the best movie ever. Certainly, Welles was never better as an actor, perhaps because the subject of betrayal, as Simon Callow has noted, was close to Welles's own broken heart. (As a teenager, Welles banished his Falstaffian father for drinking. The father duly proceeded to drink himself to death, and Welles took great care to carry the resulting guilt for the rest of his life.) Beyond his performance, Welles's direction was first-rate. The central battle scene—which begins on horseback and ends in mud, armoured limbs flailing for purchase—remains an astonishing montage of quick-cut fractal mayhem, as if someone had unpaused Picasso's *Guernica*.

For years, though, *Chimes at Midnight* was nearly impossible to find. Legal disputes prevented a proper release. Torontonians interested in acquiring a vhs recording—and, later, a dvd recording—had to make their way to abbeys like Vintage Video. The store occupied a narrow Victorian on a scenic stretch of Markham Street among other temples to physical media, like The Beguiling, a well-organized comic shop, and Suspect Video, a scruffy rental place. Condo developers would displace them all.

But for a time, you could order a bootleg copy of *Chimes at Midnight* from Vintage Video. You could order an *Eraserhead* too. Vintage Video served long-suffering connoisseurs with long memories: those hell-bent on acquiring rare or out-of-print movies. The shop tended to be quiet and devoid of customers. No radio cut the well-cultivated hush. Thus, it was impossible to be inconspicuous as you committed the violence of entering the store. Even now, I recall the trauma of easing open the disagreeable door, which my memory insists was red, heavy, and booby-trapped with sleigh bells, tambourines, and the wind-chime bones of previous, irritating customers.

The shelves and tables of Vintage Video were dense with vhs tapes and dvd cases. The organizing principle was unclear. "Genre" structured some shelves, "Director" others, but I don't recall explicit labels making the distinctions plain. In general, it was hard for your eyes to settle anywhere. (You were encouraged to pick a patch and focus.) Towards the back, you had to mount a couple steps to reach the cash. Here, the shop opened up to incorporate memorabilia of all manner. Behind the cash, a staff stairwell led up to—well, I have no idea. I assume the owner lived up there, sleeping restlessly above his movies and Sherlock Holmes statuettes. The store existed somewhere between two unpromising poles: doomed business and chilly museum. Much of the stock was expensive, and handling the collectibles, unthinkable.

The owner himself was charmingly prickly. He wore glasses and, if memory serves, a modest beard. He supplied discernment and—less valued these days—a sense of authority. One day, when I mentioned I was seeking a copy of *Humoresque*, he lit up. Apparently, this was one of the owner's favourite films. But a shadow could quickly descend. He took especially grim pleasure in confirming your worst fears about the unavailability of this or that movie. I would raise the possibility of a title, and he would bat it away. I haven't seen a copy of that in years, he would say. It was heaven.

Much of the store's stock—B-horror, pulpy westerns, musty British cinema—didn't especially interest me. But I lived for the out-of-print. The unavailable. I was especially delighted to secure a copy of Peter Bogdanovich's debut movie, *Targets*. It was a legendary salvage job. Producer Roger Corman had dangled a directorial gig—with a catch. The budding Bogdanovich had to somehow integrate existing footage of famed horror actor Boris Karloff mooning about a castle (footage that Corman owned) and then shoot additional content with Karloff (who owed Corman a couple days' work). Otherwise, Bogdanovich had absolute freedom!

Cutting the Gordian knot, Bogdanovich decided to make a movie *about* a horror actor—a kind of Karloff—who's planning to appear at a drive-in showing one of his movies. Meanwhile, a more modern breed of monster—a mass shooter—is en route to the drive-in. Cleverly, Bogdanovich relegated Corman's cumbersome existing footage to the drive-in screen. *Targets* turned out to be a love letter to the pulpy movies of the past, dispatched from the grim present. It was the cinematic distillation of Vintage Video itself.

Not everything in the store was prohibitively expensive. Scattered throughout the premises were bins of Alpha Video DVDs—budget, no-frills, un-remastered editions of obscure movies like Welles's *The Trial* or Monte Hellman's *Cockfighter*. I adored these DVDs, even if they seemed xeroxed off late-night television. You could always leave the store with something in hand.

In time, the Criterion Collection brought out a fancy, long-awaited edition of *Chimes at Midnight*. I bought it, naturally, but I held on to my earlier, grainier, hard-won copy. Today, of course, you simply punch "chimes at midnight" into the Amazon search bar to find a rental copy to stream (or, if you're a weirdo, a physical copy to own), along with hundreds of customer ratings.

That's too much input for me, though. Too much community. I miss the monastic hush of Vintage Video.

Against the Stream

SOME YEARS AGO, I went through a divorce and lived with my sister's family for a time. They went to bed early, which left me with the run of a big house in Toronto. This meant the run of the Netflix.

I had never used Netflix before. I have always been a late adopter, perhaps the last adopter—less Luddite, say, than laggard. In any case, I didn't use the platform well. Instead of scrolling through the seemingly endless rows of tiles organized into categories—"Trending Now," "True Crime," "Reality TV"—I cued up reruns of the sitcom *Community*. I even rejected Netflix's suggestions supposedly customized just for me ("Because you watched *Community* . . ."). I wanted comfort food, not a buffet addressed to catholic tastes.

The sheer volume of stuff on offer can paralyze your mind. But Netflix charges a flat fee, so you can be cavalier about your choices. The platform abets sampling and second thoughts. You can leave things half-finished on your plate—or you can binge. It's all you can eat. It's all good.

But the constant press of incoming material means you can tear through an entire season of something, sincerely enjoy it, and barely recall an episode a week later. Streamed content, as forceful and ephemeral as wind, demands about as much mental space as it does shelf space.

* * *

IT WASN'T VERY long ago you had to rent your movies or, if property was your thing, amass them gradually, one VHS tape at a time. New videos didn't simply appear, as streaming content seems to, muscling in among the mainstays because some algorithm said so. Whether you were renting or buying, you had to leave the house.

In the Age of Browsing, you had fewer choices, and you had to navigate them carefully. Unless you'd elected to make do with your cable package—or what your rabbit ears had raked from the sky—you had to accept what you found at HMV or Blockbuster. You sometimes brought home a dud, and if you'd gone so far as to buy it, you were stuck with it.

And yet none of that was a problem. My family gamely amassed its modest VHS collection, choosing from what was physically available at the store and what the studios had allowed to come to tape—that is, from what circumstance had culled for us.

My mother, especially, took to our first VCR. She bought blank tapes in bulk and recorded off cable whatever she could. A given tape had no unifying theme and contained anything from an episode of *Donahue* to a documentary about Newfoundland's religious school system (my mother was from Newfoundland). She typed out the tape's sticker on a typewriter. Each tape was a perfectly postmodern curiosity.

Because we often programmed our recordings, they were roughly hewn, edged with frayed scraps of commercials and network messaging. Eventually, my sister numbered the spines and authored a guide in a Duo-Tang. The guide made sense of the many tapes and cross-referenced their contents. The tapes came to fill a shelf in the basement.

Because we couldn't afford to buy many movies at once, we rewatched, again and again, what we'd bought or taped: *Ghostbusters*, *Romancing the Stone*, *From Russia with Love*, *I Love Lucy*, *Cheers*, *The Guns of Navarone*—a motley mix. We frequently revisited *Mildred Pierce*, a soapy piece of noir pulp; the film's bratty daughter Veda, played by Ann Blyth, never failed to scandalize my mother. Laurel and Hardy's *Sons of the Desert* always made us laugh, and *One Flew over the Cuckoo's Nest* aroused Aristotelian feelings of pity and fear.

Our little hive mind was particular, though. We loved an old British sitcom called *Are You Being Served?*, set in a department store, but only the early episodes, when Mr. Grainger was still around. We adored the films *9 to 5* and *Trading Places* (the latter, a sanitized version sans topless Jamie Lee Curtis, filched from network television) but we didn't consider their last acts successful, so sometimes we turned them off early. We knew what we liked and circled back to it, feverishly. We were an earlier people attuned to cyclical time: a merry folk revolving around its maypole.

There's great pleasure in repetition and ritual. My family came to know a lot of dialogue by heart. We anticipated the lines we cherished collectively, even if the teleplays weren't exactly "Birches." It never occurred to us to scrutinize the credits and look up the writers of these lines. Where would we have even started? There was not yet a search bar to feed names to. The critic Camille Paglia once likened the creative team behind a beloved M&Ms commercial to "folk artists, anonymous as the artisans of medieval cathedrals." The shows and movies my family adored were of similarly mysterious provenance. No algorithm had placed them before us; they described a specific constellation that we had strewn across the sky and that only we could see. A bespoke set of stars.

Our VHS collection defined a canon—and the canon defined us. For instance, a documentary called *The Art of Violin*, taped off television, introduced me to the violinist Josef Hassid, who'd had schizophrenia and perished at the age of twenty-six. Or rather: my father, by playing the documentary over and over, ensured my brain would never forget Hassid's performance of "Hebrew Melody." Years later, Hassid still seems to me the consummate cult artist, and "Hebrew Melody" the most spectral music I've ever heard.

* * *

CHOICE CAN BE oppressive, and the lack of it, liberating. The poets who still try to rhyme know this. A rhyme scheme only seems to narrow your options, forcing you into warrens that will suddenly widen, leading you to unforeseen words—and worlds. Anyway, artistic freedom is always a feint. "No verse is free for the man who wants to do a good job," wrote T. S. Eliot.

When the Prufrockian rocker Jack White came to record *Elephant*, The White Stripes' fourth album, he insisted on using Toe Rag Studios, a cramped space in London whose most modern piece of equipment was from 1963. (As the liner notes take pains to boast, "No computers were used during the writing, recording, mixing, or mastering of this record.") What's more, White imposed a deadline on himself: ten days to record. He delighted in self-inflicted limits, in wrangling an album's worth of sounds from only two guitar pedals, in recording to finite spools of tape. The sessions yielded "Seven Nation Army," an instant chestnut of stadia, its riff a trigger to mass sing-along. Constraint can be generative.

If you're a consumer of culture, as opposed to a creator of it, a lack of choice can force you to revisit the available options, even those that didn't impress you at first. Many of my favourite albums disappointed initially. Primal Scream's *Screamadelica* bounced cleanly off my brain on first listen. Had I streamed it, that might've been it. But I'd bought the CD on the advice of a record guide—a codex one sometimes consulted in the Age of Browsing— and felt compelled to give the disc another hearing. I'd made the investment, after all. I'd brought it home to live with me.

As a teenager with limited means, I often made do with what I found around the house, choosing from the finite number of cassettes that I could slot into my Walkman. I wore out my music collection, and in time turned to my sister's. Her cassettes were by mysterious outfits with names like The Smiths, The Cure, and The Jesus and Mary Chain. None of the cassettes particularly gripped me at first. The hits, such as they were, weren't always immediately obvious, and the music, stripped of context, sounded alien and bleak: spindly guitars in cavernous settings. But the trove of tapes was small, so I played them relentlessly—more out of boredom than some noble desire to give great art its due. I didn't realize I was absorbing some of the most thoughtful music recorded in Margaret Thatcher's England.

The Walkman itself was just cumbersome enough to force a modest short-term commitment. Changing tapes was a minor nuisance, and forwarding to a desired song took a toll on the battery. You were encouraged to play an album, or at least a side of it, in full. You were encouraged to give the less-immediately compelling fare a chance. To stick with it. Thus, by demanding a little bit of focus, the Walkman offered a salve for boredom.

Streaming would've offered me too easy a way out of my boredom. It would've allowed me to change my mind too quickly—to sample a few seconds of something, then toggle to something else in a matter of taps. And it's the taps, the touchscreen interfaces, that are part of the problem. The small barriers posed by physical media—loading tapes, say, or depressing buttons—hobbled us a little, slowed us down, whereas smartphones only speed us up. Nothing grows on a scrolling mind.

* * *

MANY OF MY favourite movies also required second and third chances. Like most insufferable young men, I went through a Quentin Tarantino phase. When I read somewhere that Tarantino rated Howard Hawks's *Rio Bravo* above all other movies, I sought it out—only to balk.

Here were John Wayne and a handful of deputies holed up in a jail—a dreary, spartan set, almost stock in style. They had a murderer in their charge and were waiting for the cavalry. The actors talked, joked, sang together, and only occasionally defended the jail against the advances of the murderer's gang.

What I'd missed on first viewing, waiting for the movie to dole out the least pellet of action, was some of the finest dialogue ever delivered to actors' mouths. "That's all you got?" says one character, sizing up Wayne's ragtag deputies. "That's *what* I got," replies Wayne, delivering one of the film's many classic lines, cowritten by Leigh Brackett and Jules Furthman.

That's what *I got*—a mantra for a mindset that makes do.

If the present age, the Age of Scrolling, abets sampling and second thoughts, the Age of Browsing encouraged second chances. Owning physical media forced you to reckon with it, to rewatch it, to *appreciate* it. (Maybe you sometimes tried too hard to appreciate something, but there are worse sins.) We steeped ourselves in stuff, and the stuff would start to sink in. Art has always required second—and third and fourth—chances to saturate the mind.

The mind can only marinate in so much at a time. As the poet-critic Michael Hofmann defiantly puts it,

Both one's likes and the basis on which one likes them can only be exceptions. They are personal, they are absolute, and they are nonnegotiable. And there are not very many of them. They even preclude, at times, the least curiosity or desire to add to their number.

What a liberating thought: that one's "likes" are *necessarily* limited in number; that liking less is, well, more. It's a thought that never consciously crossed my family's mind. It didn't have to. We had our canon of films, and very little could penetrate its carapace. Our likes were not the ephemeral, half-hearted kind doled out on Twitter. Our likes were "absolute" and "nonnegotiable."

Another poet-critic, Christian Wiman, is helpful here.

> Seamus Heaney has noted that if a person has a single poem in his head, one that he returns to and through which, even in small ways, he understands his life better, this constitutes a devotion to the art. It is enough. And in fact I find that this is almost always how non-specialists read poetry—rarely, sparingly, but intensely, with a handful of high moments that they cling to.

To dwell on a single poem, to the exclusion of others, isn't just okay; it's a function of devotion. To cling to a work of art—to revisit it, to steep yourself in it—is to approach the state of prayer. It's to open your mind to the possibility of being tinted. Of being transformed.

Streaming platforms, on the other hand, flood the mind. They set it afloat and bear it away—on to the next novelty. They promise abundance but deliver a deluge.

* * *

IN TIME, I moved out of my sister's house. A few years later, I remarried. My wife and I have a couple of kids, six and three, and our household subscribes to Netflix and

Disney+. But I remain a poor user of streaming platforms, except now there's the nagging feeling, shared by buffet-goers the world over, that I'm wasting good money by not consuming as much as possible. Plus, isn't there a cultural conversation to keep up with? Shouldn't I have watched *WandaVision* by now? Will I ever get back to *The Mandalorian*, which I streamed for a few episodes? Will this marquee stuff wait for me, like a wartime bride? Over two years ago, my wife gifted me with the Criterion Channel. I've yet to activate it. All these unstreamed streams are worrying. They lie about quietly, like trembling firehoses.

When I do use Netflix, I never scroll very far. The new and trending content appears near the top of the Netflix homepage. Beyond those rows, I start to feel like I'm combing a remainder bin—an unfair feeling. My inner connoisseur, ever bucking against the popular, should want the buried stuff. But the abundance of the harvest and its ephemeral character—items come and go as per the vagaries of licensing agreements—can diminish your sense of its worth. It's one big pile of leaves, whose parts are always arriving and departing.

The Age of Browsing, of course, had real remainder bins. Like the tiles on Netflix, books and tapes came and went, and if you didn't seize on your VHS copy of *Wild at Heart* (as I didn't, once upon a time) you risked losing it. But unlike the tiles, the books and tapes were physically present—and a pleasure to sift. Perhaps this is why the tiles, which constantly threaten to disappear, leave me indifferent: they'll never *really* be mine. They're pixels, and you can't possess pixels (whereas it was always a minor thrill to hurry down an aisle, scan a dense shelf,

alight on the desired spine, and finally hold the object of
your hunt).

None of this is the content's fault, of course. Blame the
surrounding digitized buffet, which lowers the prestige
of the individual lobsters. Cinephiles waited years for
someone to finish editing Orson Welles's film *The Other
Side of the Wind*. Long-suffering fans prized a precious
handful of scenes featured in a 1995 documentary about
Welles's unfinished work. But now the completed film is
just another set of pixels, next to *Squid Game* and *Selling
Sunset*.

Naturally, my five-year-old has acclimated to Netflix.
But there are only a few shows he's ever interested in.
(He, too, is overwhelmed by choice.) And there's enough
physical media lying around the house to encourage, in
his pliant mind, subversive thoughts: streaming is imper-
fect, and some content is available only on disc.

In fact, my kids have taken to an ancient ritual: Saturday morning cartoons. "CBC Kids!" they cry, as they
negotiate the narrow basement stairwell down to the TV
room. They seem to get that CBC Kids is something they
have to be on time for. And they don't mind the lack of
choice, the inability to change a mind and tap a tile. They
relax and submit themselves to the schedule. What
comes on is what they get. They make do. For now, anyway, they are swimming against the stream.

Late Adopters

SCREENS FILL OUR days, and our evenings too. Once the kids are down, we catch up on work, send emails, pay bills, and shop. We shop a lot—for groceries, birthdays, even kids' clothes. Especially kids' clothes. The kids have had the nerve to keep growing, pandemic be damned.

It's a privilege to shop safely from home and have packages delivered to your porch. (It's a privilege to have a porch!) But by the spring of 2021, a year into the on-again-off-again lockdown, I was tired of screens: of search bars, of shopping cart icons, of punching in my credit card number, which I've never quite gotten by heart. As my wife endeavoured to fill a grocery order, I would look away unhelpfully, complaining of sore eyes. I was done with scrolling.

I wrote the opening essay in this book around that time and sent it to the *Walrus*. It was originally called "On Scrolling." A *Walrus* editor retitled it, "Life in the Stacks: A Love Letter to Browsing"—a better headline that helped my humble piece go vaguely viral or, at least, interest librarians and a food editor at the *New York Times*.

More importantly, though, the new title helped me realize what I had written. You see, I thought I'd set out to register a complaint about the demands the online world makes of us. (Scrolling: A Screed.) In fact, I'd written an elegy for what seemed like a waning way of life.

I also thought I'd filed a curmudgeonly, even reactionary piece. I was surprised to see it resonate with so many readers. Apparently, there are droves of us who miss the tactile pleasure of combing through physical matter, of hefting books, of standing at a bin and clacking CDs like dominoes.

And they aren't, these droves, *just* the readers of *Walrus* essays. They are the old-souled vultures who descended on Queen Video when it went out of business in 2019, to scoop up scratched rental DVDs. (Didn't they have Netflix?) They are the snobby diehards who lined up outside Soundscapes to salvage what they could from the closing sale. (Didn't they have Spotify?) Toronto itself has seen an uptick in independent bookstores in recent years. Was the waning way of life really waning? Apparently, there's still a voting block for books, video, and vinyl. There's still a constituency that views "content" as more than just a mass of 1s and 0s suspended in the cloud.

* * *

STILL, THE CONSTITUENCY that covets physical media is a minority. Over the last few decades, the so-called market, supposedly reflecting consumer whims, has dispatched the Walkman, the Discman, the LaserDisc, the HD format, the iPod (we hardly knew ye!), record shops, bookstores, DVD rental empires, and more.

The market, to be sure, is hardly a neutral force of nature—and consumer choices aren't necessarily rational. Corporations have always had a vested interest in making us buy things we don't really need. Much as I came to like it, I did not require the CD—no one did. The cassette worked well enough. If anything, in doing away with the cassette, we lost the pleasing, anticipatory hiss of tape as it begins to travel to its new spool. The pristine CD scrubbed off that hiss and offered oodles of unnecessary storage space. Sure, it let you skip over the bloated bits of albums, but albums hadn't been particularly bloated until, well, the advent of CDs and their oodles of space! Plus, tapes were resilient. Sure, they got tangled sometimes, but the problem was rare and apprehensible. A minor, mysterious scratch on a CD, however, could suddenly befuddle your CD player's laser. Snapping a cassette in place was satisfyingly mechanical. Submitting a CD to its tray or slot was like surrendering something to a microwave. Your compact Walkman clipped onto the waistband of your pants; your round, cumbersome Discman had to stay in your hand like a discus.

But there must've been a few reactionaries who resisted the Sony Walkman when it was introduced in 1979; who felt that sitting around record players, as Mesolithic people had their fires, was the way to go. These moralists would've pointed out that the Walkman encouraged anti-social behaviour: it isolated you from the society of others. They would've also pointed out that music sounded better on vinyl. And they would've been right—would still be right. Digital music formats, like the CD, have an antiseptic precision. Vinyl, on the other hand, has depth. Warmth.

On the fortieth anniversary of the Walkman, Alan Cross, a Canadian radio host, recalled that his first pair of pre-Walkman headphones, "an ugly beige set from Koss with a long, coiled cord, weighed close to five pounds. I was always conscious of that tonnage on my head." Who would turn their nose up at the lighter headphones of the Walkman era? Who would pooh-pooh progress?

Still, I like to think there were a few grumpy holdouts, who believed in their bones that music sounded better when it weighed down your skull.

* * *

EVERY PARADIGM HAS its stubborn loyalists, those who hold out as long as possible before embracing the next paradigm. One name for these holdouts is "late adopters." A positive reading is that they're prudent consumers. They're biding their time, weighing their options, keeping an eye on *Consumer Reports*, and waiting for the market to pick a winner.

But they also might be lazy, bad with change, comfortable with the available options, or tired of the relentless demands to upgrade. On October 19, 2021, one Julian Oliver, an educator and activist, tweeted:

> Not upgrading your hardware until it is beyond repair or truly inhibiting your process/work is a pro-planet, pro-human rights, anti-extractivist act of resistance.

I found this tweet—which had been liked over twelve hundred times—enormously nourishing, even if my own persistent failure to upgrade my tech is a sign of sloth and incompetence. Now, more than ever, we need to push back on the ever-encroaching entreaties of Big Tech. As Melville's Bartleby very nearly said, "I would prefer not to install the update."

I have great sympathy for late adopters. I have especial sympathy for their most doomed manifestations. Take George Minafer, the bratty conservative in Orson Welles's *The Magnificent Ambersons*. The film takes place in the early twentieth century, but George is a throwback to the nineteenth. He likes his ballrooms, his cotillions, his horses lashed to buggies. The picture pits Minafer against Eugene Morgan, who's trying to bring an iteration of the automobile to market. Minafer, played by Tim Holt, is shrill and grating. ("Get a horse," he chides from the vantage of his horse-drawn sled, as he laps Morgan's stalled prototype.) Meanwhile, Morgan, played by Joseph Cotten, is warm and charming. It's an error in casting, really; Welles was a romantic deep down, and his movie's sympathies were meant to lie with the unlikeable throwback. The late adopter.

* * *

I CERTAINLY SYMPATHIZE with George Minafer when I visit Starbucks these days, where I duly line up to buy my drip coffee, which is how civilization taught me to do it, only to watch a gaggle of young people storm in to collect their online orders: drinks already made and paid for, sweating on a small counter dedicated to their kind. Meanwhile, the analogue line to the cash has inevitably ground to a halt. The young people are caught up in some noisy drama; they don't give the line-waiters like me a second thought. The line-waiters, though, are acutely aware of the young people, who *appear* to have jumped the line. In fact, the young people had the presence of mind to order through their Starbucks app, or whatever, before setting out. The young people, scrollers at heart, had the app to begin with, whereas I use my smartphone sparingly, for email and Twitter, and download virtually nothing onto it, least of all coffee apps, because I know how to get coffee—or thought I did. I look around. The other line-waiters are inevitably my age or older.

Every era has its George Minafers. They aren't quite nostalgists, casting their gaze back on the past; the Minafers are still living *in* the past. They can do so because the ever-evolving present still makes available enough of the past for the Minafers to continue their lives as is, at least for a little while longer. They can still line up to place their order in person, browse a mall, walk through a bookstore, purchase the film on DVD, and feed a CD to the slot their aging model of car maintains. But the window, a slo-mo guillotine, is always closing on the Minafers.

* * *

A MOMENT OF silence for those Minafers whose Black-Berry devices finally stopped working on January 4, 2022.

* * *

AFTER AN EVENING of mayhem and rape, *A Clockwork Orange*'s Alex—played memorably by Malcolm McDowell in Stanley Kubrick's 1971 film—pleads illness and skips school for the day. He turns up at a music store—or what passes for one in Kubrick's future—and flips through vinyl records while chatting up two young women. It's a dystopia of roving gangs and Brutalist architecture. But it still stocks physical media.

Neal Stephenson's 1995 novel *The Diamond Age*, however, imagines a different future, in which nanobots or "mites" fill the air like soot and matter is compiled at the click of a button. Hence the very literal title: in a world where molecules can be snapped together like Lego, diamond is bound to be ubiquitous.

Early in the book, a couple of urchins discover a scrap of old-school cloth, which only the wealthy can afford. Nell watches in awe as her brother Harv—working with toothpicks, a "flashlight in his teeth"—teases out a thread.

"How many does it have?" Nell said.

"Nell," Harv said, turning to face her so that his light shone into her face, his voice coming out of the light epiphanically, "you got it wrong. It's not that the thing has thread *in* it—it *is* threads. Threads going under and over each other. If you pulled out all of the threads, nothing would be left."

The urchins decide that mites must've made the scrap of cloth. "It had to be mites, Nell, nothing else could do it."

There's no need to browse in a world with matter compilers. But one's sense of history, one's worldview, can start to narrow. Similarly, a world with smartphones leaves us both empowered and oddly blinkered, blinded like poor Nell. Simple things and practices, from which we've separated ourselves, become sources of wonder. What would my small children make of Sam the Record

Man, if we could bend time and beam them back, among the rows and rows of CD bins?

* * *

WILL THE YOUNG people of the future even have stuff? Do they have stuff now?

Some years ago, while planning a trip to Japan, my wife and I tumbled into a very specific and narrow rabbit hole: YouTube videos featuring Westerners walking around Tokyo, talking to their cameras. In some cases, the vloggers were tourists; in others, they were expats who'd clearly made a life in Japan. The vloggers panned their cameras across shelves in conbini (convenience stores), experimented with vending machines, and zoomed in on their ramen. All were young, and all had evolved the same charmingly scrappy style: their cameras jounced as they walked, and their videos were jagged with jump cuts. They seemed to be the most amiable of amateurs.

The first red flag should've been the comments. Some of these rough-hewn videos (which were little more than diaries filmed on foot, lacking all narrative shape) had attracted hundreds, even thousands, of comments. We must've chalked that up to virality; clearly, other viewers with an interest in Japan had made some of these videos into hits. But when my wife and I, scrolling idly, landed on one of these vloggers' home pages, we were shocked to discover that the vlogger had hundreds of thousands of subscribers. One young couple in particular, Anthony and Kalel, turned out to be some sort of power couple on YouTube, with millions of followers between them. (Alas, they have long since broken up.)

These were "influencers," apparently. They made sponsored videos touting this or that product. They appeared at conventions and submitted themselves to selfies with their fans, the fans waiting in long winding lines. Some of the influencers had product lines—merch with their names on it—but physical stuff was hardly the point. They were *content creators*. They shared their feelings, took their viewers on walks, conducted taste tests, unboxed deliveries, dared to consume ghost peppers, demonstrated makeup applications, or executed DIY crafting. Some of them attempted skits or pop songs, but you couldn't exactly buy a DVD or CD of the performances. Our attention was the primary product, duly sold to advertisers. The smartphones, it turns out, were browsing us.

* * *

STUFF, TO BE sure, can be a nuisance. Books, CDs, and DVDs fill our shelves and follow us in moving vans. They take up space in our lives; they become a *part* of our lives. Still, I'm scandalized by the example of those who don't seem to need physical media: the scofflaw downloaders (I've known a few), the e-book enthusiasts, the relentless de-clutterers, and the happy-go-lucky streamers with their heads in the cloud—among so many others. All these types have turned away from tactile stuff with dismaying ease. Perhaps they have chosen a more enlightened and minimalist mode of being. Perhaps they want to pay less (or not at all) for their content.

On the one hand, I don't blame the partisans of the digital—of the *diffuse*—for not valuing content enough to want to possess very much of it in physical form. I don't blame them for their indifference. Didn't our professors teach us that works of art are products of ideology? That taste is a construct? Surely the sheer ubiquity of the word "content" signals the triumph of a certain strain of post-modernism, which sought to dissolve hierarchies of taste and wrangle everything from novels to TV shows to cereal boxes under one levelling label: "text." The move from "text" to "content," then, is merely a mutation, a variant of the virus. Beethoven, The Beatles, BTS—it's all just 1s and 0s. Every digital file gets its fifteen minutes of fame. Warhol would've been crazy about Wi-Fi.

For my part, I've always needed the works of art that matter to me to be *near* me. I've needed my stacks of CDs, DVDs, and books to lean on—and take care of. I'm the hall monitor in the house, who flips over the abandoned disc so that the vulnerable, scratchable side faces the ceiling. I'm the bleeding heart who feels for the paperback's fissured spine.

I feel less steady without my stuff. By "stuff," I don't mean the mundane material goods we accumulate through shopping—new clothes, kids' toys, the tchotchkes our homes are choking on. (I don't mean the matter we need to Marie Kondo.) Nor do I mean the mindlessly stockpiled wealth that's meant to shore up an insecure identity, like the crated treasures that Charles Foster Kane hoards in *Citizen Kane*. I mean the stuff that matters, that gives our lives meaning.

Our choices, really, are chisels. What we choose to surround ourselves with helps define those selves. We are what we love.

* * *

BROWSING, OF COURSE, will continue—in some attenuated form or other. William Gibson's 2014 novel, *The
Peripheral*, offers a brief glimpse of twenty-second-century browsing. Gibson posits a future in which climate
change, war, and pandemics have seen to much of the
world's population, leaving a small and largely wealthy
class of people. These survivors pilot "peripherals"—
robots, basically—from the comfort of their homes. But
they still, the pilots, get out from time to time.

At one point, Wilf Netherton, a publicist, takes a walk
with a friend in London. The friend is at the wheel of a
peripheral, a "fairy prince in a flat tweed cap." Netherton
is in the flesh.

> Streetlights were coming on. Goods were on offer,
> in the windows of shops staffed by automata, by
> homunculi, by the odd person either present or
> peripheral. He'd known a girl who'd worked in a
> shop near here, though he couldn't recall the street,
> or her name. . . . They were passing a shop in which
> a Michikoid in riding habit was folding scarves.

What a relief, to know that browsing bricks-and-mortar
shops might still be a thing in twenty-second-century,
post-apocalyptic London, even if some of the retail asso-
ciates aren't precisely human.

Do Amazon drones deliver goods to the porches in
Gibson's world? Does Jeff Bezos's brain linger in a
life-support vat? *The Peripheral* is frugal with the details
it releases to its reader. (Gibson's worldbuilding tends to
be oblique.) My sense is that browsing, as Gibson imagines it, becomes a niche activity. An exotic luxury. But

then perhaps it already is. Gibson has always written about the present by proxy of some sci-fi future. He has always seen the apocalypse in plain view.

* * *

PERHAPS I'M MERELY mourning the loss of a paradigm because it happened to be the one I grew up in. I was born in 1978, a year before the Walkman. I had no investment in vinyl or sitting around the communal record player to share a moment of music with others. Nor did I have a say when Sony's co-founder, Masaru Ibuka, decided he wanted an easier way to transport his music, a whim that left us with the Walkman in the first place. No one expected the Walkman, a rich man's toy, to be a hit. Sony anticipated it would sell five thousand units a month; it sold fifty thousand in its first two months alone.

In other words, I came to consciousness in a world that allowed you to carry The Beatles between your ears. The Walkman was perfectly normal, as natural a part of the infrastructure of life as pipes carrying water, except Sony's device carried music. I was indifferent to other, older worlds and their backward peoples.

The youngsters in the Starbucks, swanning in to collect their orders while the rest of us Minafers moulder, are indifferent too. They are comfortable with their phones in a way that I will never be. They summon their drinks, movies, videos, vlogs, and music at will. Let a thousand buildings crumble. They were born to scroll.

But they, too, will be left behind by the zeitgeist. Maybe some of them will come to mourn their obsolete smartphones even as they decry the latest, buggy release of Apple's artificial eyes, the devices that will beam movies directly into the brainpans of the late twenty-first century. Maybe the moony, arty, old-souled youngsters of the decades to come will balk at implants. Maybe they will pine for the rustic elegance of a touchscreen interface, for the bygone pleasure of scrolling a screen with a fleshy, non-robotic thumb.

Maybe the late adopters of the future are already among us.

Coda:
A Program
of Resistance

LET'S BE CLEAR: I'm not immune to the pleasures of a smartphone or the convenience of streaming. Scrolling the internet turned up some useful material that fed this book.

And I'm not suggesting some better way to navigate information on a screen. I assume Zuckerberg et al. have sorted the screens out. That is, I assume that scrolling, by way of flicks of finger, is the best option we have until our smartphones leap the divide, pass through our pupils, and take up in our brains.

But the internet is as riven, in its way, as the scraps of ancient papyrus museums display—you just can't see the lacunae. Many albums and movies can't be streamed and lie stranded in physical formats, in the tar pit of the past. Hyperlinks to pieces I wrote only a few years ago have already rotted like rope bridges. Software updates have futzed with the formatting of old essays. Pages have simply vanished.

Nevertheless, digitization cheerfully promises a paperless future of infinite storage. Interventions like the Wayback Machine endeavour to archive the ever-proliferating pages of the internet. But there's no guarantee a web page or digital file will persist. Paper will always be a safer bet than PDFs. A paperless future would be a dystopia.

So, I buy books from bricks-and-mortar shops when I can. And CDs and DVDs, too, though the stores that stock these have dwindled. Mostly, I try to slow down, which, really, was the benefit of old-school browsing in the first place. Browsing couldn't be done with the flick of a thumb. It plunged you into your entire body and set the body afoot, sometimes for hours, with no smartphone to check—and no easy way for others to check in. Browsing was calibrated to the natural pace of a body moving through space. It was good for your cardiovascular health. (Scrolling, on the other hand, is hard on your eyes.)

Browsing forced you to reckon with physical media, to wander among aisles and stacks that didn't presume to know your preferences and weren't so insidiously jostling for your attention. You could pause, eye a spine, and tip some strange compact sliver of the world towards you. Only the mildest of inputs—the background noise of the store, say, or the muffled car horns of the street—competed for your interest. You were exquisitely alone.

Solitude—a strain of it—is still available for a little while longer at least. Bricks-and-mortar bookstores have rebounded in cities like Toronto. Meanwhile, many of the smaller Ontario locales my family loves to visit have maintained an institution or two that still believes in physical media. Mill Street Books in Almonte is a charming shop that keeps a small but well-curated selection of new vinyl. ZAP Records in Cobourg is dense with CDs, records, and old music magazines. A few steps down the street from ZAP, Let's Talk Books makes room for comics (at the very back of the store, where the local youth may browse and brood) and a discerning selection of magazines, including my beloved *MOJO*. And, of course, the very publisher of this book runs its iconic bookstore in Windsor. Serendipity is finding a way to nurture many of the young minds outside of the metropolis.

I don't offer a program of resistance except to say: when culture is a literal click away, you should want to slow down and conjure some hurdles, make consumption a gradation harder. Cut down on your web-based content, maybe. Balk at the bingeable. Use the internet, if you must, but as a delivery system. Go ahead and buy those expensive Criterion DVDs. Go ahead and order the Japanese import. Don't bookmark, print out. Revel in what arrives in the good old mail—and spurn what comes too easily. Avoid Amazon. Stream the album, but if you like it, buy the physical format. Take care of your things. The Compact Disc is not a coaster, so grip it by its edges, and, when setting it down, leave the shiny side face up. Play your kid the original 1977 theatrical release of *Star Wars* on discontinued DVD. (Don't stream the airbrushed version on Disney+.) Seek out first editions, rare albums, out-of-print movies, old numbers of magazines someone took the care to shrink-wrap. Read the liner notes. (Smell the liner notes; no one is looking.) Second-guess your decision to downsize your physical media. Be careful not to cart your memories to the curb. (Please know, though, that I will help you unload them for a good price.) Don't break the spines of books. Don't download the app. When not in lockdown owing to a global pandemic, visit bookstores and record shops, and often. Arrange to forget your smartphone and contrive to be alone.

You will be amazed at what lies just out of view of the scroll.

Notes

"Browser History"

Entries in Online Etymology Dictionary and a blog called the *Etymology Nerd* by Adam Aleksic gave me the roots of the words "browse" and "browser."

A Wikipedia article on window-shopping led me to *Perceptions of Retailing in Early Modern England* (2007), by Nancy Cox and Karin Dannehl, and the September 1938 issue of the *Rotarian*, containing William Moulton Marston's thoughts on window shopping.

The Jeff Guo quote comes from an article called "The Secret Feminist History of Shopping," which appeared in the *Washington Post* in 2016.

A 2020 *New York Times* obituary confirmed that Larry Tesler was the first to apply the term "browser" to a software search system.

A *Washington Post* article by Jessica Goldstein, from 2012, offered useful background on the Melody Record Shop.

"In Praise of the Mall, Boredom, and Just Browsing"

I found some of the information about the current state of malls and department stores in a 2020 CNBC article by Lauren Thomas. Some of the stuff on Victor Gruen and the rise of malls came from an article by Josh Harmon and Exa Zim on insider.com. I also consulted Wikipedia and a *Star Tribune* article dated October 7, 1956, archived via newspapers.com.

I found the stuff on boredom being good for the brain in a 2020 *Forbes* article by Bryan Robinson, which references the work of the neuroscientist Dr. Alicia Walf.

A 2017 *Guardian* article by Paul Lewis gives voice to some of the regretful engineers who made our devices so addictive by, e.g., designing shit like the "pull-to-refresh" function.

"An Elegy for Effort, Memory, and Passion"
The interview with Liam Hayes was conducted by Jason P. Woodbury and appeared on the website Aquarium Drunkard in 2018.

"I Remember the Bookstore"
The only online scrap I could find to prove the existence of The Book Company at Sherway Gardens was on a blog called the *Fangirl Files* and a Reddit thread by the owner of the blog. I salute her.

"Second Spin"
An article by Brian Baker for streeter.ca about the closing of Vortex Records offered handy background on the late store and its curmudgeonly owner.

"Three Elegies for Bricks and Mortar"
An article by Muriel Draaisma for cbc.ca featured material on the demise of Soundscapes. A profile by Tim Davin in *Taddle Creek* provided some background on Phil Liberbaum.

I got some insight into Spotify's algorithm from a 2020 piece in *Analytics India Magazine* by Sameer Balaganur. A 2017

piece in *Wired* by Libby Plummer introduced me to the idea
of Netflix's "taste groups."

"Against the Stream"

Some of the information about The White Stripes' embrace
of constraint while recording *Elephant* was found in an article by Oliver Newland and Anthony Sfirse on happymag.tv.

"Late Adopters"

I stumbled on some useful content about the history of the
Walkman in a *Time* article by Meaghan Haire. A post by Alan
Cross on globalnews.ca, occasioned by the fortieth anniversary of the Walkman, supplied a fascinating eye-witness
account of the terrible weight of pre-Walkman headphones.

Acknowledgements

EARLIER VERSIONS OF some of the essays in this book originally appeared in *Slate*, the *Walrus*, and the *Yale Review*. A fragment from "I Remember the Bookstore" appeared in the *Dark Horse*. Thanks to the original editors: Sam Adams, Carmine Starnino, Meghan O'Rourke, Jill Pellettieri, and Gerry Cambridge.

Thanks also to my publisher, Dan Wells. This book was his idea, and his quarrels with the manuscript made it better.

JASON GURIEL IS the author of several books, including the verse novel *Forgotten Work* (Biblioasis 2020). His writing has appeared in *Air Mail*, the *Atlantic*, *Slate*, the *New Republic*, the *Yale Review*, the *Walrus*, *Poetry*, and elsewhere. He lives in Toronto.